The 20 British Prime Ministers
of the 20th century

Chamberlain

GRAHAM MACKLIN

HAUS PUBLISHING • LONDON

First published in Great Britain in 2006 by
Haus Publishing Limited
26 Cadogan Court
Draycott Avenue
London SW3 3BX

www.hauspublishing.co.uk

Copyright © Graham Macklin, 2006

The moral right of the author has been asserted

A CIP catalogue record for this book is available from the British Library

ISBN 1-904950-62-0

Designed by BrillDesign
Typeset in Garamond 3 by MacGuru Ltd
info@macguru.org.uk

Printed and bound by Graphicom, Vicenza

Front cover: John Holder

Contents

Prologue: Chamberlain's Character, Outlook and Image

In 1967, nearly 30 years after his death, Lord Salter observed that as a historical figure Neville Chamberlain presents, 'a problem of personal assessment of unusual difficulty. The personality is so deeply submerged under the policy for which he bore the first responsibility … the feelings towards him, and the opinions about him of his contemporaries, were so divergent and so passionate that the man himself, his real nature and quality, will be hard to recapture and convey.'[1] Robert Self, editor of the four volumes of Chamberlain's diaries and letters, observes that Chamberlain, an essentially sensitive and private man, deliberately obscured his deeper personality by cultivating a 'hard defensive shell' which protected a shy, sensitive, fragile character deeply wounded by the barbs of personal criticism, although, with its hard, abrasive aloofness, this defensive mechanism has ultimately proved detrimental to his historical reputation.[2]

There is certainly some truth in this observation, although within the parameters of this brief sketch it impossible to do more than correct a few of the more enduring misconceptions. Even in his own day Chamberlain was regarded by some as irredeemably parochial, a petit bourgeois *arriviste*, 'a mean and callously fraudulent small tradesman', forever armed with his trusty umbrella into which, in David Low's satirical cartoons, he gradually metamorphosed. To his friends this portrayal of dreary mediocrity was 'a travesty of the facts which is in the worst possible taste'.[3] It is an image that has endured, however, thanks in large part to the well-publicised observations of his contemporaries. Clement Attlee observed that whilst Baldwin's mind was 'tuned to the national wavelength', Chamberlain's 'never got beyond Midland Regional'.[4] Lloyd George concurred, spitefully regarding Chamberlain as 'a good mayor of Birmingham in an off year'.[5] 'A nice man,' thought Harold Macmillan though, 'very, very middle class and very, very narrow in view.'[6]

This negative image was hard to dispel, particularly when his forbidding exterior was added to the balance. Chamberlain cut a prim and rather austere figure, resembling his father physically. 'Black-haired, heavily moustached and corvine in profile, it was his misfortune that even when he most wished to be amiable his face seemed to wear a sneer,' observed one commentator.[7] The wife of the right-wing journalist Collin Brooks was 'convulsed by his likeness to Groucho Marx, the film comedian'.[8] His dress, even by the standards of the day, was positively Edwardian and led to his being nicknamed 'the coroner',[9] an appellation that he shared with another Conservative politician who chronically misjudged Hitler, the German Chancellor Franz von Papen.

Chamberlain's sartorial austerity was complemented by his thin, grating voice, which exuded 'a quality of harshness' and was 'without seductive charm'.[10] Although Chamberlain was famed as a brilliant and incisive debater, he was no natural orator and found public speaking an ordeal. Indeed Chamberlain was deeply envious of his half-brother Austen who 'sits in an easy chair, reads a chapter or two of a novel, scribbles a note or two and goes to sleep – and his speech is made'.[11] Chamberlain's speech, though lucid and precise, was clipped, unemotional and lacked rhetorical flourish, which he despised, but as a result of which his speeches were rather dry and mechanical. As Lord Templewood observed: 'this indifference to rounded periods and carefully considered statements was the very antithesis of Churchill's resounding eloquence. Unlike Churchill, he did not sufficiently appreciate the need for purple patches and inspiring perorations in a period of great emotional strain.'[12] Indeed Chamberlain's 'prose without wings' contained an element of 'asperity' that 'often gave the impression of harshness, greater than he intended'. As a result 'he riled the more because he seldom slipped; he had command of himself and exercised it sharply'.[13] Chamberlain's abrupt and domineering manner hardly endeared him to his parliamentary colleagues.

As a newly-arrived secretary in Downing Street John 'Jock' Colville found Chamberlain had little time for small talk and 'seldom said to me anything not strictly related to business'.[14] Chamberlain was a technocrat *par excellence* who derived satisfaction from 'administration' rather than 'the game of politics'. Political theatricality as practised by opponents including Lloyd George left him cold. Although frequently castigated for his lack of political imagination Chamberlain's administrative skill was *sine qua non*. As one historian surmised, Chamberlain, 'may not have been a painter of the political canvas with the visionary strokes of the broad brush, but he did had an unmatched grasp of pointillist detail and of the practicalities of a set composition'.[15] Indeed Chamberlain's keen analytical mind and intimate knowledge of the minutiae of both Cabinet and committee procedure, combined with a razorlike precision and prodigious memory, made him an exacting taskmaster and formidable political opponent. As R A Butler remembered, 'by nature and by intention his approach to political problems was the exact opposite of Baldwin's. Whenever I thought of this approach I always found myself comparing it to a "ton of bricks". Talking to him day after day about statements and answers in the House I got to realise that, if one phrase or one word were out of place, an order would be given and the builder's lorry would be tipped, and if one didn't watch out the ton of bricks would descend on one's own head.' Chamberlain's exactitude made him appear brusque to the point of being rude when conducting parliamentary business. 'He frequently redrafts in pencil with very little hesitation and very little crossing out,' Butler continued, 'He does not like vague and polite phrases but wishes to go straight at the Opposition and express exactly what he means. The traditional soothing of Members by such phrases as "the honourable and gallant gentleman will be aware" is usually erased.'[16]

Nowhere was this more evident than in his hostility to his Labour colleagues for whose *lamentable stupidity* Chamberlain had nothing but contempt. Such sentiments sat ill at ease with Baldwin's conciliatory tone, not to mention his attempts to foster industrial harmony, leading Baldwin to admonish his Chancellor for his intolerance. Chamberlain was unrepentant. *The fact of the matter is that intellectually, with a few exceptions, they are dirt*, he wrote to his sister.[17] Chamberlain found it increasingly hard to hide his disdain, particularly for Liberals like Gilbert Murray whose moral superiority drove him to distraction.[18] 'In the Commons itself, where I used to sit next to him,' noted R A Butler, Chamberlain 'could not conceal his impatience with the Labour and Liberal leaders. He would fidget and fume expletives in a manner which brought to my mind the famous physical eccentricities of Dr Johnson.'[19] The disdain Chamberlain felt for the Labour benches, increasingly prevalent towards the climax of his political career, prevented him from becoming a truly 'national' leader when he became

Prime Minister in 1937; it certainly hastened his downfall in 1940.

Polite but little more, Chamberlain also appeared incapable of forging intimate personal relationships with his Cabinet colleagues, few of whom were at ease with him. Reserved if not downright awkward in his personal dealings with close colleagues, those outside the Cabinet found his manner positively glacial. The backbench MP Cuthbert Headlam found him 'a cold fishy creature who puts your back up in five minutes' not least because he was lacking any noticeable 'spark of humanity'.[20] Lord Vansittart found him 'a Personality without *allure*'.[21] This was an observation verily attested to by Conservative party chairman J C C Davidson. 'Temperamentally, I disliked him,' recalled Davidson, 'he was a man who did not draw sympathy out of the individual with whom he was dealing or conversing ... It was really not a test of knowledge or intelligence, but a test of personality – everyone was attracted to Bonar Law and to Baldwin, and nobody was attracted to Neville Chamberlain.' Admittedly Davidson was not a neutral witness, yet there was much to be said for the mischievous anecdote he was fond of recalling, allegedly made by a Birmingham party activist: 'If you cut the – in half he wouldn't bleed.'[22]

Chamberlain's lack of personal charisma, not to mention his resolutely 'unclubbable' nature, contrasted sharply with that of younger, debonair politicians like Anthony Eden or Duff Cooper whose personal standing within the Conservative Party was extremely high. As such he had no widespread popular support within the party. As Headlam observed laconically, although Chamberlain was ultimately assured of succeeding Baldwin, he was 'not so popular that he cannot be kept waiting'.[23] As his own obituary remarked, Chamberlain's refusal to 'bandy civilities' meant that he was 'more cut off than any Prime Minister or party leader should be from the rank and file of his followers and from the fluctuations of current opinion; and it was a common and a just belief that closer links with the world outside Whitehall would have strengthened him as a democratic leader.'[24] His half-brother Austen was particularly concerned by this apparent personality defect. 'Boiled down, it all comes to this. Neville's manner freezes people ... everyone respects him and he makes no friends,' lamented Austen.[25] He 'knows nobody' opined Lady Oxford, widow of the late Liberal Prime Minister Herbert Asquith.[26] Chamberlain's diffident self-confidence, often mistaken for conceit, arrogance or worse, was a veneer almost penetrated by Labour leader Walter Citrine who noted perceptively that 'his reserved nature made it difficult for him to become intimate with anyone, and undoubtedly much of his outward frigidity was due to a disturbing self-consciousness.'[27] 'When I was Prime Minister,' wrote Stanley Baldwin shortly after Munich, 'I always had Neville, as Ramsay had me, to interpret my views to the Cabinet and carry them along. The trouble is, Neville has nobody.'[28] From the other side of the looking glass Chamberlain made an almost identical observation, though his loneliness was compounded by the fact that there was no one upon he could rely due to that fact that his colleagues' abilities were *meagre in the extreme* and exuded little promise.[29] Even his relations with his own half-brother, though cordial, were never warm, leaving a certain distance between the two men, exacerbated by their political disagreements. This inability to foster close working relationships threw Chamberlain back upon his own reserves of self-sufficiency, fuelling his autocratic tendencies, a serious portent for the future direction of British politics.

Unsurprisingly, given his fastidious, pedantic manner, Chamberlain had not the least time for the frippery of high society. Even dinner was a trial, not least because he preferred to work in the evening. The prospect of social engagements filled him with a sense of grim foreboding and those he did attend he found *inexpressibly tedious.*[30] He was only taught to waltz with great difficulty and no doubt under some duress.

'Boiled down, it all comes to this. Neville's manner freezes people … everyone respects him and he makes no friends.'

AUSTEN CHAMBERLAIN

He was particularly disdainful of social events in the provinces, particularly those in his own constituency to which he reacted with scornful snobbery: *Do all people of cultivation go to London or what is the explanation?*[31] Contemptuous of such wanton frivolity, Chamberlain found personal gratification in solitary leisure pursuits like horticulture, his interest in which was rewarded with election as a fellow of the Royal Horticultural Society. Chamberlain dedicated hours to the careful cultivation of orchids and wild plants, many of which he donated to Kew Gardens when the burdens of office denied him the time to devote the necessary attention to them. Aside from botany Chamberlain was passionate about natural history, entomology and was a particularly keen ornithologist. Even whilst Prime Minister Chamberlain could still find time to rattle off a note to *Countryman* about a *perfect specimen* of leopard moth he had discovered in the Downing Street garden.[32]

Indeed, in many respects Chamberlain was far more the 'countryman' than Baldwin. He loved outdoor pursuits, especially pheasant shooting which, after 1937, he enjoyed in the company of the King on Balmoral moors, and moreover of angling, in particular the art of fly-fishing, which he was taught by former MI5 officer Sir Joseph Ball – *a better fisherman than I* – director of the Conservative Research Department from 1930 until 1939. Thereafter Chamberlain indulged his passion during his Easter holidays under the tutelage of his friend Arthur Wood with whom he fished on the river Dee at Cairnton every year from 1922 until the latter's death in 1935. Brooding over the complexities of who should be appointed Minister of Defence in early 1936 Chamberlain's mood lightened considerably having discovered his new Parliamentary Private Secretary Lord Dunglass had *excellent salmon fishing on the Tweed*.[33]

Culturally, Chamberlain's aesthetic taste tilted naturally towards the classical rather than the modern, detesting the likes of Stanley Spencer and Jacob Epstein whose work he believed positively degenerate. He enjoyed instead the works of Gainsborough and the painters of the Italian Renaissance, making frequent tours of the National Gallery in the company of its director, Sir Kenneth Clark, who helped him select a number of paintings for his Downing Street residence. Chamberlain read avidly and, despite the demands of office, found the time during April 1937 to devour modern novels like *Gone with the Wind*, which *greatly impressed* him.[34] As he grew older Chamberlain took increasing pleasure from the music of Bach, Schumann, Mozart, Chopin and his favourite, Beethoven, whose quartets *take one to another world*. Unlike Hitler Chamberlain did not care for Wagner.[35] He felt the Italian conductor Arturo Toscanini was *in a class by himself* though he regarded the Russian composer Sergei Rachmaninov as *a little second rate*.[36] Chamberlain had no high regard for opera, however, *with the exception of Mozart's*. He also enjoyed the films of Charlie Chaplin at whom *we laughed till we ached*. The theatre was another particular pleasure, especially Shakespeare whom Chamberlain studied diligently, often quoting apposite passages in response to ministerial queries. He had a particularly profound knowledge of Hamlet though he found John Gielgud's portrayal as *much too noisy* for his tastes.[37] During the Phoney War period Chamberlain found the time to *methodically* reread all Shakespeare's comedies. *One must have something to take one's mind off these perpetual war problems and the unending nagging of the Press & the House of Commons*, he recorded.[38] Chamberlain's cultural tastes may be considered catholic and perhaps predictable for a man of his age and class but his understanding of them was profound rather than provincial.

Part One

THE LIFE

Chapter 1: Early Life

Neville Chamberlain was the only son of the second marriage of Joseph Chamberlain, son of a Camberwell cordwainer who, having amassed a fortune manufacturing screws, entered politics, rising to epitomise the Victorian imperial ethos as leader of the Liberal Unionist Party and then Colonial Secretary in the Conservative government. Chamberlain's first wife had died giving birth to their son, Austen, who later became Foreign Secretary, and five years later Chamberlain remarried his wife's cousin, Florence Kenrick. Neville was born a year later in Edgbaston, Birmingham on 18 March 1869. The young Chamberlain grew up in an atmosphere of fervent Unitarianism, within a close-knit, happy family, surrounded by cousins, but his mother died when Neville was six and his father, devastated, retreated into political life leaving his children at Highbury in the care of his two sisters. Chamberlain was never entirely at ease with his father and his relationship with his half-brother Austen, six years his senior, was built on respect rather than affection.

In 1882 Chamberlain followed Austen to the prestigious Rugby School. He was decidedly unhappy there. Shy and withdrawn, Chamberlain was bullied and beset by loneliness, compounded by a lack of affection from his Aunt Clara when he returned home. His father evidently felt that further 'classical' schooling was wasted on his youngest son and

Neville did not follow Austen to Cambridge University or indeed on the European tour, judged a prerequisite for any aspirant political career. Neville was not fated to go to university at all though he undoubtedly possessed the intelligence, a fact belatedly recognised by his father who observed in later life that Neville was 'the really clever one'.[1] Instead, in 1886, Neville was enrolled at Mason College, Birmingham reading science, metallurgy and engineering, subjects chosen for him, in preparation for a career as a captain of industry though he also developed a voracious interest in natural science, devouring the works of Darwin, Huxley and Wallace. After completing his education he joined a chartered accountancy firm and, although offered a permanent post, his chosen career was prematurely terminated in 1890 by a massive slump in the Argentinean economy, which threatened the Chamberlain family with financial meltdown.

In 1874 Joseph Chamberlain had sold the majority of the family's assets, invested them in South America and lived off the interest. Chamberlain saw a way out of the impending crisis following a conversation with Sir Ambrose Shea, the Governor of the Bahamas, which persuaded him that he could recoup his losses by growing sisal, a plant with stiff purple leaves from which high-quality hemp could be made. Chamberlain promptly reserved 20,000 acres and dispatched his sons Austen and Neville to Nassau to investigate the prospect of what promised to be a 30 per cent return on his investment. Greatly pleased by his sons' report, in May 1891 the Colonial Secretary dispatched his youngest son to the remote Bahamian island of Andros to personally supervise the undertaking, which was supposed to be largely self-managing. It was a comparatively primitive existence, one which Chamberlain embraced with enthusiasm although his personal letters increasingly reflected a sense of having been condemned *to a life of total solitude, mentally if not physically*.[2]

For an all too brief moment, however, it appeared that all the backbreaking toil and privation was worth it and that the 'Andros Fibre Company' would become a prosperous concern, reinvigorating the family's fortunes. But Chamberlain's initial optimism was misplaced. Sisal plants simply would not grow on Andros and those that did were of poor quality. In April 1896 after five years of hard toil Chamberlain ruefully conceded defeat. Full of self-reproach he wrote to his father that:

I no longer see any chance of making the investment pay. I cannot blame myself too much for my want of judgement. You and Austen have had to rely solely on my reports but I have been here all the time and no doubt a sharper man would have seen long ago what the ultimate result was likely to be.[3]

Instead of replenishing the family coffers Andros cost Joseph Chamberlain £50,000 though he understood that the financial loss was nothing compared to the loss felt by his son. The 'seven thousand acres of worthless land' that Neville left behind was sold in 1921 for £200 and used to purchase a French cabinet. It was a poor return for having wasted the best years of his life.[4] Chamberlain returned to England in 1897 diminished by a sense of personal failure. It was not a failure entirely of his own making, however, and certainly not one for which he bore the sole responsibility.

Having returned to England Chamberlain's personal fortunes were reinvigorated through family connections. Two uncles, Arthur and Walter, both prominent Midlands industrialists, swallowed whatever private reservations they may have had concerning their nephew's financial acumen and arranged for him to be appointed director of Elliott's

Metals Company based in Selly Oak and which manufactured ships' sheathing. Chamberlain was also made manager of the Bordesley-based firm Hoskins & Sons, manufacturers of ships' berths and which, in this fiercely competitive local industry enjoyed a distinct advantage over its two nearest rivals by holding the patent for folding berths which allowed for the transportation of emigrants on the outward journey and cargo on the homeward voyage. Chamberlain was also appointed to the board of the Birmingham Small Arms Company with the assistance of his uncle, Herbert, who was the firm's chairman. Through such enterprises, *I shall be transformed from a colonial into a provincial*, Chamberlain joked.[5]

Chamberlain soon established himself as a leading industrialist in Birmingham. He intimately involved himself with the minutiae of company business which meant that he was well regarded by his employees because he 'would listen to an office boy's complaint, had learned all the detail himself, knew men by name, would instantly pick out one who looked ill, send this one to hospital or pay for another's recuperation at the sea'.[6] This enlightened attitude perhaps emanated from his proximity to the shop floor. Chamberlain had sole control of Hoskins, a small firm with no more than 200 employees, and often considerably less, meaning that 'there was no great gulf between the skilled craftsmen and the small owner, and Neville was always close to his men.' Despite Chamberlain's other business concerns, ' … it was to Hoskins' that he gave most of his time, and he found a deep satisfaction in proving that on his own he could survive.'[7] The importance of this period in Chamberlain's early life should not be underestimated. The success of Hoskins' helped facilitate Chamberlain's psychological recuperation in the immediate aftermath of his return from the Bahamas, restoring his self-confidence after the failure in Andros.

Chamberlain was unusually progressive as an employer:

he recognised the value of trade unions and encouraged and facilitated their development. He instituted a worker's surgery, welfare supervisors, and in 1914 war benefits for injured employees and bereaved dependants. He also introduced production bonuses and a pension scheme. In many ways Chamberlain was a model employer. His success also coincided with the emergence of similar beliefs to those which had informed his father's social vision. He was a staunch proponent of slum clearance programmes, town planning and other initiatives, many of which he helped institute, which he genuinely believed would alleviate the plight of the urban working classes.

Chamberlain's success in local business served as a springboard for his involvement in the public life of Birmingham itself. He played an active part in the Chamber of Commerce, became a magistrate and was intimately involved in the affairs of Birmingham University of which his father was the first Chancellor, raising both funds and the profile of the newly invested institution. He was a member of Birmingham General Hospital's management board, treasurer of Birmingham's General Dispensary and was involved in many other acts of public philanthropy. His social thinking led him to devise a hugely successful scheme to remove the burden of trivial outpatient cases from the General Hospital, prefiguring Lloyd George's own National Insurance Act. It also showcased many of the administrative attributes that made Chamberlain such a success in local government.

1911 was a pivotal year for Chamberlain both personally and professionally. In January, having just turned 41, Chamberlain married Anne Cole de Vere after a brief courtship. The daughter of an Irish sporting family, on paper their characters were mutually exclusive – he precise and meticulous, she impulsive and emotionally volatile – and yet their marriage was a long and happy one. One wonders what Chamberlain thought of his gregarious brother-in-law Horace, a notorious prankster who caused numerous scandals in the 1930s with his practical jokes, which included listing 'fucking' as his recreation in *Who's Who*. After their marriage the couple moved to Westbourne, Edgbaston, which was to be their home for the remainder of their lives. Later that year she bore him a daughter, Dorothy and two years later a son called Frank.

1911 was also significant as the year Chamberlain changed his mind. Living in the shadow of his father and older half-brother, Chamberlain showed little inclination towards a political career beyond serving as honorary secretary of the city's Liberal Unionist Association. As a young man denied his youth, Chamberlain desired wealth not political power. *I never had any intention of standing in S. Wolverhampton or anywhere else*, he wrote to a friend. *The fact is, I was intended by nature to get through a lot of money. I should never be satisfied with a cottage, and having chucked away a competence – you know where – I am going to toil and moil till I grub it back again.*[8] Chamberlain had previously spoke on his father's behalf campaigning for tariff reform after he left the government in 1903 but, other than declaring himself *an*

Austen Chamberlain (1863–1937) was Secretary of State for India 1915–17, and Chancellor of the Exchequer in Lloyd George's peacetime coalition. He succeeded Bonar Law as Conservative Party Leader on Law's first retirement in March 1921, but resigned in October 1922 after the Carlton Club meeting broke up the Coalition. He was Foreign Secretary in Baldwin's second government 1924–9, negotiating the Locarno Pact in 1925 and winning the Nobel Peace Prize. He was briefly First Lord of the Admiralty under the National Government in 1931. He was the only 20th-century Conservative leader never to be prime minister.

ardent adherent of his father's cause, Chamberlain's political activities extended no further. Indeed, a further round of speechifying in 1906 on behalf of the Tariff Reform League was only undertaken, *sorely against my will*.[9]

The idea of entering politics had been germinating in Chamberlain's mind since the announcement of the Greater Birmingham Bill, which promised to transform Birmingham into 'the second city in the Empire'. And Chamberlain, who shared his father's belief in the transformative power of municipal service, ardently desired to be a part of it. *If this is confirmed by Parliament I shouldn't like to be outside the administration* recorded Chamberlain.[10] Chamberlain sincerely sought to alleviate the desperate and squalid conditions in which many of its citizens still lived. Birmingham's infant mortality rates were such that in 1899 they reached 199 per thousand. Even in 1911 diseases such as tuberculosis were rife. In November 1911 Chamberlain successfully stood as a Liberal Unionist rather than a Conservative candidate. This was not an unimportant distinction for it meant that Chamberlain was never strictly a 'Conservative' MP. Indeed Chamberlain certainly never saw himself as such. His reformist views on domestic policy were nearer to those of the Fabian socialists than his Conservative colleagues, something that he acknowledged himself after becoming Prime Minister in 1937:

> *I recall that I myself was not born a little Conservative.*
> *I was brought up a Liberal and afterwards a Liberal*
> *Unionist. The fact that I am here, accepted by you*
> *Conservatives as your Leader, is to my mind a demonstration*
> *of the catholicity of the Conservative Party, of that readiness*
> *to cover the widest possible field which has made it this great*
> *force in the country, and has justified the saying of Disraeli*

that the Conservative Party was nothing if it was not a National Party.[11]

Despite being *in* rather than *of* the Conservative Party, Chamberlain was duly elected, on a manifesto emphasising town planning, improved transport and technical education, to Birmingham City Council as representative of All Saints Ward and was appointed first chairman of the

Town Planning Committee and member of the Public Health and Housing Committees. Under Chamberlain's tutelage the first two town planning bills in Britain were passed in 1913. His rise in local politics was meteoric. The following year he was elected alderman and in 1915 Lord Mayor, following in the footsteps of seven relatives who had previously held the office. The Lord Mayor was *ex officio* a member of every committee of the Corporation and Chamberlain strove to attend as many meetings as he could, quickly becoming intimately connected with almost every aspect of the Corporation's municipal work. His reforming zeal was such that he worked tirelessly to alleviate the conditions of the poorest and most desperate, earning him the goodwill of local Labour councillors, which survived his later antipathy to the Labour movement. His concern for the plight of the urban poor did not diminish, evident in his distress at seeing the poor physical state of evacuee children in 1939.[12]

One of Chamberlain's most enduring achievements was the City Orchestra (later the City of Birmingham Symphony Orchestra) founded in 1919. In 1916 he had been greatly moved by a performance of the Hallé Orchestra and resolved that a city of Birmingham's stature was deserving of its own orchestra. Chamberlain's social ethos imbued its foundation, which was made possible by funding the venture from the rates. This innovation ensured that cheaper seats broadened the accessibility of music whilst also making the orchestra to some extent self-funding.

He also pioneered another initiative that greatly benefited the city, the Birmingham Municipal Bank (BMB), a local city-run bank for ordinary citizens founded despite opposition from the joint-stock banks, which proved so successful that it was made permanent by an Act of Parliament in 1919. During the course of 1915 the government sought to persuade its reluctant citizens to invest their wages in war loans. Chamberlain believed that this could be achieved through municipal savings associations, which would encouraged people to save (their contribution being deducted from their wages at source) but which, in return for guaranteed interest, forbade them from withdrawing their savings until the end of hostilities, released this money for use as a war loan. Despite opposition from trade unions and the Treasury Chamberlain's determination saw his proposal become law in 1916. The BMB continued its unique existence until it was taken over by the TSB in 1976.

Chapter 2: Westminster, Birmingham and Back

Whilst Chamberlain busied himself with municipal affairs in December 1916 his half-brother Austen sought to elevate Neville to national politics by commending him to Lord Curzon for the post of Director-General of National Service after the Liberal MP Edwin Montagu turned it down. When Neville was subsequently offered the post by Lloyd George (leading him to resign as Lord Mayor of Birmingham) Austen was ecstatic. Austen was also understandably apprehensive at the 'gigantic task' now facing his half-brother, who had no parliamentary experience, becoming, 'like a hen with one chick and more anxious about him than I have ever been about myself'.[1]

In essence Chamberlain's job was to recruit volunteers for essential war work. Chamberlain's tenure was not a success, however. His department failed to alleviate the manpower problem. After eight months only a few thousand volunteers were found. Inexperienced and with no seat in the House of Commons from which to lobby for support Chamberlain's position was hardly helped when Lloyd George took an almost instant dislike to him. Crestfallen, Chamberlain resigned on 8 August 1917. Lloyd George greeted the news with a palpable sense of relief: 'Neville Chamberlain has resigned and thank God for that.'[2] For Lloyd George the failure of the national service department was 'specially disappointing' because 'instead of being a unifier of competing interests, it became merely an additional department dipping into the pool of civil labour; and instead of allaying, it tended to increase the industrial discontent which prevailed'.[3] Another of Chamberlain's colleagues, William Bridgeman, though not unsympathetic, explicitly blamed Chamberlain for the failure. 'Nothing in my mind can excuse him for filling his dept. with a huge crowd of officials before there was work for them, many of whom were notoriously incompetent,' observed Bridgeman, who also complained that Chamberlain displayed, 'a good deal of petty animosity ... which surprised me, after all I had heard of his ability. I cannot believe that he is anything like as good a man as Austen.'[4] The majority of his parliamentary peers were less harsh in their judgement, however, recognising that Lloyd George had placed Chamberlain in an invidious position. Speaking during the course of the debate Conservative Party leader Andrew Bonar Law referred to the 'absolutely impossible task' Chamberlain had faced. 'The allusion to Neville,' noted Austen, 'was warmly cheered all over the House. There is a general recognition of the fact that he never had a fair chance.'[5]

'The allusion to Neville was warmly cheered all over the House. There is a general recognition of the fact that he never had a fair chance.'

AUSTEN CHAMBERLAIN

Suitably aggrieved, Chamberlain believed Lloyd George had treated him abominably and thereafter developed an *unconquerable distrust* of the *dirty little Welsh Attorney* who, as he advised Churchill in 1940, would perform the role of *Marshal Petain*, if Germany successfully invaded Britain.[6] This enduring sense of loathing was readily reciprocated by Lloyd George who later drew a venomous but broadly accurate portrait of Chamberlain, (then Chancellor of the Exchequer), in his *War Memoirs*, as a man of 'rigid competence' who was 'indispensable for filling subordinate posts at all times,' but was, 'lost in an emergency or in creative tasks at any time'.[7] The enduring animus between the two men was such that Chamberlain actively opposed Lloyd George's return to government thus relegating the latter to the political margins from where he continually sniped at his former protégé. 'More's the pity,' Austen noted of their private feud, 'for together if they were together they might do a great deal.'[8]

It was a depressing period for Chamberlain whose crushing sense of personal failure was compounded by lingering memories of the Andros debacle. Chamberlain's despondency deepened when only weeks before Christmas his cousin Norman, with whom he had worked closely on Birmingham City Council, was reported missing in action in France. It was an agonising time for the Chamberlain family and particularly Neville who rated Norman as *the most intimate friend I had*. Indeed, although Chamberlain had virtually given up hope, when the grim confirmation of Norman's death arrived the following February it was nevertheless a terrible blow. *Oh, I am sick at heart*, he lamented.[9] Norman's death, and that of another cousin John the same year, left an indelible mark upon Chamberlain, occasioning his only book, *Norman Chamberlain: A Memoir* (1923). More importantly it strengthened his visceral aversion to war and fortified his commitment to public service. No longer was Chamberlain preoccupied by his desire to *grub back* his lost fortune. *I could not settle down to make money, much as I should like to be rich*, he wrote in August

I could not settle down to make money, much as I should like to be rich. When I think of Johnnie and Norman, I feel I could not back out of public work of some kind.

CHAMBERLAIN

1917, *When I think of Johnnie and Norman, I feel I could not back out of public work of some kind.*[10]

Thus, despite the failure of his first foray into national politics, Chamberlain stood during the 1918 general election in Ladywood, Birmingham. Chamberlain's confidence had been severely dented by his bruising contretemps with Lloyd George and he secretly confided to his sister his belief that his career was already over. *My career is broken*, he lamented on the eve of his election to Parliament, *How can a man of nearly 50, entering the House with this stigma upon him, hope to achieve anything? The fate I foresee is that after messing about for a year or two I shall find myself making no progress …*[11] Elected as a member of the Birmingham Unionist Association, Chamberlain's radical reforming politics was regarded as 'wild' by his half-brother Austen whilst Chamberlain regarded him as *unprogressive and prejudiced.*[12]

Chamberlain's pessimism surrounding the perceived stagnation of his parliamentary career was perhaps responsible for his decision to turn down an under-secretaryship in March 1920. His fortunes were transformed, however, on 19 October 1922 following a meeting of Conservative MPs at the Carlton Club which precipitated the fall of the Lloyd George coalition, and which offered Chamberlain the opportunity for rapid advancement. Bonar Law appointed him Postmaster-General, though Chamberlain only accepted having assured himself that Austen, who had backed the losing side, would not be offended by his preferment. His appointment was renewed in February 1923 and the following month Bonar Law appointed Chamberlain to his Cabinet as Minister for Health. Chamberlain thrived in the post and was responsible for a plethora of socially progressive legislation including the Rent Restriction Act and the Chamberlain Housing Act aimed at providing adequate housing for working class families via the provision of subsidies for their construction and which provided the foundation for Labour's Wheatley Housing Act in 1924. Less than ten months later the new Prime Minister, Stanley Baldwin, appointed Chamberlain Chancellor of the Exchequer.

Baldwin's first ministry was a brief affair. On 25 October 1923 he called a general election on the issue of protectionism and a general tariff only to be defeated by Ramsay MacDonald's equally short-lived Labour administration. Baldwin returned to office after the October 1924 general election during which Chamberlain defended his Ladywood seat against a youthful and ruthlessly ambitious Labour candidate, Oswald Mosley, who harried Chamberlain on a range of issues including the Rent Act over which he accused Chamberlain of being the 'landlords' hireling'. Chamberlain was incensed by the accusation and demanded that Mosley retract it *as a gentleman*. Mosley, however, was no gentleman. He was, in Stanley Baldwin's delicious phrase 'a cad and a wrong 'un and they shall find out'. And they did in 1932 when Mosley founded the British Union of Fascists. During October 1924, however, the vigorous tenor of Mosley's campaign momentarily looked as if it might

Sir Oswald Mosley (1896–1980) first entered Parliament in 1918 as a Conservative, but then sat as an independent before joining the Labour Party in 1924. He was eventually returned for the Birmingham constituency of Smethwick in 1926, a seat he held for Labour until he resigned from the government and founded the New Party in 1930, which became the British Union of Fascists in 1932. Interned during the War for his links to Italian and German fascism, he attempted a comeback in 1950s Britain, but retired from politics in 1966 and lived in exile in Paris until his death. (See *Life&Times: Mosley* by Nigel Jones.)

succeed. 'A new radical Joe had come to Birmingham,' noted Mosley's biographer, 'with all the fire and enthusiasm so conspicuously lacking in the original's desiccated successors.'[13]

But it was not to be. The publication of the Zinoviev letter four days before the general election on 29 October, coupled with a wider loss of faith in MacDonald's administration, propelled the Conservatives to victory. In Ladywood Chamberlain narrowly beat Mosley by 77 votes but only after several recounts. 'A downpour of rain washed the lifeless body of the last of the Chamberlains back to Westminster,' lamented Mosley with reference to the heavy thunderstorm that had allegedly caused many Labour voters to stay at home.[14]

During the party's brief period in opposition Chamberlain emerged as a forceful exponent of the 'New Conservatism' – Baldwin's response to Labour's emerging electoral threat that enabled him to reassert his 'moral authority' over the party – which Chamberlain articulated through *Looking Ahead; Unionist Principles and Aims*, the main tenants of which formed the basis for the party's election manifesto in October. Back in office Baldwin sought to appoint Chamberlain as Chancellor of the Exchequer. Chamberlain, however, believed that whereas he might make *a great Minister of Health* he would only ever be a *second-rate Chancellor* and requested to return to the Ministry of Health. Chamberlain was also acutely conscious that unless the Conservatives *leave our mark as social reformers* Labour would soon relieve them of the accoutrements of power and so was determined to give substance to Baldwin's 'New Conservatism'. He immediately embarked upon an ambitious programme of social reform in the arenas of housing, health, local government, the extension of national insurance and widows' pensions. By 1929 Chamberlain had proposed 25 pieces of progressive legislation, 21 of which became law, providing the foundations upon which

Labour's Welfare State rested. However, against a backdrop of resistance from party managers who feared they would antagonise vested interests, two of Chamberlain's greatest achievements, the reform of both local government and the Poor Law system, were only pushed through with Baldwin's support towards the end of his administration.[15] As one commentator has observed of Chamberlain's administrative prowess, 'under his guidance, the confused and complicated patchwork of local government was entirely rationalised by 1929 with a commanding sweep which – put to a different goal – would have been the envy of any totalitarian planner.'[16] Only 40 years later did another Conservative government feel the urge to tamper with Chamberlain's vision.

With unemployment rising to one million, something the Derating Bill, the government's last legislative gamble, failed to alleviate, and the Conservative Party slowly losing its grip on power Baldwin called a general election for 30 May 1929. The Conservatives' uninspiring slogan 'Safety First' failed to resonate with the electorate and Labour, although lacking an overall majority, now emerged as the largest party. Baldwin conceded defeat and resigned as Prime Minister. Although he found himself out of office Chamberlain secured re-election in the safe seat of Edgbaston, which he retained until his death, and that winter embarked upon a tour of East Africa. When he returned in March 1930 Chamberlain founded and chaired the Conservative Research Department (CRD).

The Conservatives' defeat in the general election unleashed a wave of recrimination against Baldwin emanating predominantly from the Right who regarded him as a 'semi-socialist' whose moderate centrism had brought the Conservative Party low. This assault on Baldwin's leadership ran from November 1929 to March 1931, becoming particularly acute during September 1930, and was exacerbated by the 'Empire Crusade' of two media moguls, Lords Beaverbrook and Rothermere, who arrogantly demanded that the Conservative Party adopt the very protectionist platform that had led to its defeat in 1924. Chamberlain, dispirited by the morose torpor into which Baldwin's leadership had sunk, was also fearful lest the Prime Minister's unpopularity tarnished his own reputation because of their working synergy. Nevertheless Chamberlain remained loyal throughout, working diligently for a rapprochement between Number 10 and the press barons.[17] His efforts betrayed, Chamberlain was *bitterly humiliated and outraged* to learn the press barons had been playing a double game, mollifying him with *soft words* whilst covertly working to capture local Conservative associations and influence their MPs in favour of tariff reform. If Chamberlain's loyalty had faltered this humbling experience probably pushed him back towards Baldwin not least because Beaverbrook *has destroyed my confidence in him and when that has happened I don't readily give it again vide L.G.*[18]

The chief casualty of the mounting crisis, however, was not Baldwin but his close friend J C C Davidson, the Conservative Party Chairman whom Chamberlain thought *a fool and a danger in his post* and against whom he had been conspiring to replace with his own candidate since April.[19] Over the course of a tense and 'unpleasant' luncheon Chamberlain persuaded Davidson to fall on his sword in order to relieve the pressure on the beleaguered Baldwin.[20] It was not his original intention but Chamberlain replaced Davidson as chairman of the Conservative Party on 23 June 1930, causing consternation in some quarters given his pronounced lack of personal skills.[21] Towards the end of the crisis, on 1 March 1931, Chamberlain presented Baldwin a memorandum written by Robert Topping, the party's chief agent, arguing that it was widely believed that Baldwin's standing was so low that 'in the interests of the Party ... the Leader should reconsider his position'. Topping's memorandum handed Chamberlain, who believed Baldwin's position was fast becoming irretrievable, the perfect weapon with which to usurp him. Chamberlain was fearful, however, that bringing Topping's memorandum to Baldwin's attention would be interpreted as evidence of his desire to unseat the Premier for his own advantage and so consulted widely before doing so. Shaken from his lethargy, Baldwin momentarily considered resigning. *The Times*, believing he had, prematurely printed his political obituary. Fortified by Lord Bridgeman Baldwin rallied, however, and fought back against the press barons at the Westminster St George's by-election where his candidate defeated Beaverbrook's, occasioning Baldwin's ringing rejoinder to the press barons' desire for 'power without responsibility – the prerogative of the harlot throughout the ages'. With Baldwin's authority restored Chamberlain lost the chance to force the pace of events. Baldwin would step down only when he was good and ready.

There was little respite for Baldwin. No sooner had he restored his authority within the party than, as Chamberlain put it, *things suddenly boiled up in the City*.[22] By the summer of 1931 Britain was faced with a looming financial crisis caused by the collapse of the banking system in Central Europe leaving the City of London dangerously exposed which, coupled with a prospective budget deficit of £120 million, threatened a serious run on the nation's gold reserves, diminishing the value of sterling. Heavy borrowing from financiers in Paris and New York only narrowly averted disaster. The Bank of England advised the government that these loans would only be forthcoming if the government could restore overseas confidence by balancing the budget. The bankers insisted that confidence would only be restored through swingeing economies in government spending, particularly in unemployment benefit. Chamberlain, who monitored the situation on Baldwin's behalf whilst the latter returned to his holiday in Aix-les-Bains, France, was firm in his mind that retrenchment was *the vital thing* and insisting upon cuts totalling no less than the £96.5 million recommended by the May committee on national expenditure, a figure which included £66.5 million in cuts to unemployment benefit. Financial crisis precipitated political crisis and on 24 August 1931, following his Cabinet colleagues' refusal to assent to such economies, MacDonald liquidated his second Labour administration and, at the King's bidding, became head of the 'National Government', an all-party coalition whose Cabinet included both Baldwin and the Liberal leader Sir Herbert Samuel.[23]

To say that Chamberlain was 'the constructive engineer' of the National Government is certainly an exaggeration.[24] Indeed Chamberlain (like Baldwin) was extremely sceptical of a coalition, perceived as unnecessary and undesirable, writing to his sister, *I myself hate the idea and hope it wont come to pass.* As Shadow Chancellor it was Chamberlain's resolute insistence that MacDonald accepted the economies demanded by the City or effectively forfeit Conservative support that proved instrumental in determining the initial parameters of the government's response to the crisis. Although Chamberlain had accepted the grave seriousness of the crisis, with many, including his own half-brother, predicting that the 'deluge' was only 'a matter of hours away,' in terms of being able to manipulate events to the Conservatives' own advantage Chamberlain could only advise a reluctant Baldwin to support a MacDonald-led coalition in the belief that it was a strictly short-term expedient that needed to be supported *for the sake of the country*. Thereafter it would be business as usual. All this rather contradicts the idea that Chamberlain was ruthlessly pursuing a sinister design aimed at wrecking the Labour Party, a notion dismissed as 'patently absurd'.[25]

In terms of long-term strategy, however, Chamberlain was markedly successful in impaling Labour 'on a series of ever more difficult hooks of financial policy', forcing Snowden to adopt the large-scale fiscal reforms demanded by the Conservatives and the City, whilst preventing a rise in the level of direct taxation, which would disproportionately affect the rich, the Conservatives' natural constituency.[26] It was not therefore simply a question of balancing the budget but as Chamberlain acknowledged, balancing it in the right way. To this end the Conservatives induced their Labour partners to adopt the doctrine of 'equality of sacrifice', convincing them that the unemployed too had to shoulder their share of the burden. By spreading the burden of responsibility for the cuts the Conservatives were able to deflect unpalatable accusations that an 'upper class' government was foisting 'economies' on the most vulnerable sectors of society. Such an accusation would be extremely damaging to the Conservatives electorally, particularly in the north. The grinding privation these measures caused was captured with heartbreaking poignancy by Walter Greenwood in *Love on the Dole* (1933) and by George Orwell in *The Road to Wigan Pier* (1937) and was bitterly resisted not least by sailors at Invergordon who mutinied rather than accept the cuts, provoking panic in the City and a massive outflow of gold from London leading ultimately to Britain being taken off the Gold Standard despite a promise, only days earlier, that sterling was 'as good as gold'. Although it was not a conscious conspiracy on Chamberlain's part for the Conservatives the formation of the National Government proved a most fortuitous occurrence since it forced Labour to adopt the twin pillars of Conservative economic orthodoxy, economies and protectionism.[27]

Chapter 3: Backbone of the Government

Although the pretence of a 'National' Government was retained during the 1931 general election, the Conservatives won a landslide victory over MacDonald who was now tied to the mast of a ship over which he had little control. Chamberlain replaced Phillip Snowden as Chancellor of the Exchequer, quickly establishing himself as the backbone of the National Government, though this was almost cut short by an acute attack of gout in 1932. Having recovered, Chamberlain stamped his authority on the National Government's financial policy. He continued with Snowden's austerity-minded measures, encapsulated in his first notably severe budget of April 1932, in the belief that only through economies could the budget be balanced, financial reserves restored, and stability and confidence re-established. Although his approach to financial matters was pedestrian, the near national bankruptcy of 1931 had transformed such orthodoxy into an 'article of faith' – one to which Chamberlain adhered for all its faults. Chamberlain is frequently castigated for his lack of vision. In some ways this is irrelevant. The economy began to revive from early 1933 and continued to do so for the remainder of the decade.[1]

One Chamberlain's first acts as Chancellor was to protect the home market by introducing the Abnormal Importations Act and then at the beginning of 1932 a general tariff of 10 per cent aimed a filling the deficit in the balance of payments, raising further revenue to stabilise the currency and thus reduce unemployment. This piece of legislation was widely seen to be the realisation of his father's long cherished ambitions. As Chamberlain told the House of Commons: *There can have been few occasions in all our long political history when the son of a man who counted for something in his day and generation has been vouchsafed the privilege of setting the seal on the work which the father began but had perforce to leave unfinished.* At the end of this emotional speech Austen Chamberlain strode from the Treasury bench to shake his half-brother's hand amidst rapturous applause.[2] A significant omission from the general tariff was goods from the Commonwealth, which, it was hoped, would be resolved at the Ottawa conference in Canada to be held later that summer. Alas for Chamberlain, the Dominion governments were far less interested in imperial preference than in protection for their own markets. Imperial trade was not reinvigorated at Ottawa which only really achieved a declaration of intent from all concerned that the reduction and eventual elimination of tariffs between the Dominions, as had been proposed at Ottawa, was a step in the right direction.[3] Having weathered the economic storm Chamberlain could declare during the passing of his 1934 Budget that, *we have now finished the story of* Bleak House *and are sitting down this afternoon to enjoy the first chapter of* Great Expectations.[4]

> *We have now finished the story of* Bleak House *and are sitting down this afternoon to enjoy the first chapter of* Great Expectations.
>
> CHAMBERLAIN

As the decade progressed Chamberlain stamped his authority on matters of defence and foreign affairs too. As Chancellor Chamberlain dominated the policy of both the National Government, and, though his chairmanship of both the CRD and the Cabinet Conservative Committee, that of the Conservative Party too. By 1934 he had already developed serious misgivings about the increasingly infirm MacDonald – *woolly* and *out of touch* – not to mention the concept of the National Government itself.[5] Nevertheless, he continued to work tirelessly on its behalf frequently from 9.30 a.m. to 1.30 a.m. *Long after S.B. has gone to bed*, he noted pointedly. His workload was immense. *Every day one interview or Committee succeeds another and in the evening there is generally a box large enough to keep me out of bed till the small hours. It is strenuous work but I suppose that I would not willingly change it now for any other.* Even in bed he found it hard to wind down and when he woke, *as one must do several times in the night my thoughts rush inevitably to the problem. But I have trained myself sufficiently to be able to force them off it at once and in a few minutes I am asleep again.*[6] Chamberlain's was a restless mind, compelled to purposeful activity. Writing from the Treasury to his sisters in May 1934 whilst trying to grapple with the proceedings of the Disarmament Committee Chamberlain noted that *in my office the amount of work you have to do largely depends on what you make for yourself. Unhappily it is part of my nature that I cannot contemplate a problem without trying to find a solution.*[7] Such a disposition drew Chamberlain into an array of policy decisions outside his portfolio and soon led him to conclude that he was the organisational and administrative dynamo powering the National Government. Writing to his sister in June 1934 he commented: *You would be astounded if you knew how impossible it is to get any decision taken unless I see that it is done myself and sometimes I wonder what would happen to this government if I were to be smashed up in a taxi collision.*[8] As Chancellor of the Exchequer Chamberlain's eye ranged over an astonishingly wide assortment of subjects leading him to view himself as having become *a sort of Acting PM – only without the actual*

power of the PM. I have to say 'Have you thought' or 'What would you say' when it would be quicker to say 'This is what you must do'.[9]
Despite his emerging as the pivotal figure in the National Government, when MacDonald finally conceded his inability to govern it any longer in June 1935, the reigns of power passed not to Chamberlain but to Stanley Baldwin.

By this point Chamberlain was immersed in the question of rearmament, however. It is one of the ironies of history that Chamberlain's reputation is stained with the opprobrium of being one of the 'guilty men' who failed to rearm Britain when throughout the 1930s he was depicted by Labour as a 'war monger.' Indeed the revulsion towards war caused by the Great War was such that Britain's transition from a disarming to a rearming state remained painfully slow despite increasingly shrill warnings about the scale and pace of Germany rearmament. In this respect the formation in February 1934 of the Defence Requirements Committee (DRC) chaired by Sir Maurice Hankey, which reported to Cabinet that Germany was now Britain's 'ultimate potential enemy', was something of a landmark. Chamberlain's close advisor, Sir Warren Fisher, the Treasury's permanent secretary, recommended that the DRC should only consider proposals relating to defence expenditure once they had been fully reviewed by the Chancellor, a decision that rankled with, though ultimately was accepted by, both the War Office and the Admiralty. At a stroke Chamberlain became the supreme arbiter of the nation's defences, holding the purse strings and thus dictating the parameters of the debate surrounding the scale and direction of the rearmament drive.

Chamberlain was not inclined either by temperament or desire, particularly in the aftermath of the Wall Street crash, to embark on a vast spending spree. Indeed, his first act was to present Treasury figures for defence estimates lower than at any time since the First World War. Chamberlain's priorities were clear: *Today financial and economic risks are by far the most serious and urgent that the country has to face, and that other risks have to be run until the country has had time and opportunity to recuperate and our financial situation to improve.*[10] The idea of spending £85 million on defence was to Chamberlain a *staggering prospect.*[11] Concerned to balance the budget and reprieve some of the cuts of the 1931 budget, Chamberlain succeeded in whittling this down first to the £76 million recommended by the DRC and then to £50 million. The War Office for instance was forced to accept £19 million instead of £40 million spread over five years. By providing such a paltry sum Chamberlain was effectively ruling out military intervention on the Continent and 'advertising the strategic outlook that would make appeasement inevitable later in the decade'.[12]

Ironically, whilst the Air Ministry prevaricated over the pace of aerial rearmament it was Chamberlain who pushed for the expansion of the Royal Air Force (RAF). The rise of air power had engendered a strategic revolution that leaders like Baldwin were not slow to grasp. 'When you think of the defence of England you no longer think of the chalk cliffs of Dover; you think of the Rhine. That is where our frontier lies,' Baldwin told the House of Commons in July 1934.[13] Chamberlain agreed, concluding that, in the absence of collective security, *we shall be more likely to deter Germany from mad dogging if we have an air force which in case of need could bomb the Ruhr from Belgium.*[14] Despite being a voluble proponent of RAF expansion Chamberlain had to defend himself at the party conference against a motion, re-tabled from the previously year and thus meant as a rebuke, demanding rearmament. Conceding that imperial defence *had reached a dangerously low level*, Chamberlain blamed *successive Governments for the last eight and a half years*, which, he pointedly reminded his audience, included his most vociferous critic, the former Chancellor Winston Churchill.[15] From the sidelines Churchill, armed with information secretly provided by a former MI6 officer Desmond Morton, head of the Industrial Intelligence Centre, on the real state of preparedness of the *Luftwaffe*, appeared to be a lone voice calling for aerial rearmament to maintain, as a bare minimum, parity with Germany.

Chamberlain was not unsympathetic to such calls in principle and indeed raised the Air Ministry's proposal for a further 52 bomber squadrons to 80, with the DRC settling upon 75. *I have really won all along the line*, he observed.[16] Following a Cabinet meeting in July 1934 'Scheme A' was agreed whereby Britain would increase the number of squadrons to 84 by March 1939 at a cost of £20 million, a figure which, including the Fleet Air Arm and overseas defence, meant 1,465 aircraft. Attempts by Air Ministry to bring forward the date from 1939 to 1936 were effectively blocked by Chamberlain on the grounds that *there was nothing in our information in regard to German preparedness to justify the proposed acceleration*. Chamberlain also warned his colleagues of the potentially disastrous consequences of incurring *fresh commitments*, as he saw them.[17] Chamberlain was not going to be railroaded into profligacy by anyone though as the campaign continued he suffered fearful visions of *cranks* and *experts* who, given half a chance would be *merrily doling out subsidies in every direction*. He promised his sister *we shall do nothing rash*.[18] By the end of 1935 Chamberlain was only too aware that his attempt to steer a middle course *between rigid orthodoxy and a fatal disregard of sound principles and the rights of posterity* had

I don't really care much what they say of me now so long as I am satisfied myself that I am doing what is right.

CHAMBERLAIN

made him unpopular though he was completely impervious. *I don't really care much what they say of me now so long as I am satisfied myself that I am doing what is right*, he wrote.[19]

Chamberlain's continuing commitment to rearmament can be judged by the March 1935 *Statement Relating to Defence*, which highlighted the perils of German rearmament and announced that British defence expenditure could 'no longer be safely postponed'. To this end an extra £10 million to the defence budget backed the White Paper. Hitler reacted to the announcement with a *childish exhibition of bad manners*, cancelling a meeting with Sir John Simon and Anthony Eden scheduled for the following day. More importantly Hitler countered with a public announcement that Germany, in direct contravention to the Treaty of Versailles, would create a *Luftwaffe*, something it had been doing secretly for some time. Such news bolstered Chamberlain's belief that the publication of the White Paper was *necessary and timely*.[20] On 16 March Hitler introduced conscription, creating overnight an army of half a million men. *Hitler's Germany is the bully of Europe*, Chamberlain lamented in light of these developments, dispatching Sir John Simon to Berlin to *talk plainly* to Hitler warning him that if Germany failed to accept France's offer of bilateral non-aggression pacts with its Eastern neighbours Europe would coalesce into rival, armed camps.[21] The visit was a bitter disappointment and Simon returned with nothing but 'a series of negatives' in response to British proposals. *What are we to do next?* wondered Chamberlain.[22] Although Hitler rejecting any form of multilateral agreement with France, who subsequently signed a mutual alliance pact with the Soviet Union, to the horror of Whitehall, Chamberlain was consoled to hear that Hitler did not wish to challenge British naval supremacy, leaving the door ajar for the conclusion of the Anglo-German Naval Pact under which Germany committed herself to a fleet no greater than 35 per cent of the tonnage of the Royal Navy (excluding, remarkably, submarines), allowing Britain to maintain, or so it thought, command of the seas, the cornerstone of Imperial defence.[23] The conclusion of the Anglo-German Naval Pact was every bit as important to Chamberlain's appeasement strategy as the development of a formidable British bomber deterrent because Britain gained the strategic space to begin *making eyes at Japan*. In doing so Chamberlain sought to neutralise a potential enemy (and in doing so defraying the cost of refitting the fleet to defeat it), restore the balance of power in the Far East and in doing so safeguarding British interests, giving himself a freehand to concentrate on resolving European affairs. Chamberlain's oft-quoted remark that *it is always best and safest to count on* nothing *from the Americans except words*, was not the insult Churchill later painted it to be but rather a particularly prescient analysis that nothing short of *an attack on Hawaii or Honolulu* would rouse America to come to Britain's aid.[24]

Delighted with the outcome of the Anglo-German Naval Pact, which he believed to be almost too good to be true, Chamberlain was nevertheless aware that it meant nothing so long as Hitler pursued aerial supremacy over Europe, which, if achieved, would render British security dependent upon German goodwill.[25] Given these cold facts Chamberlain was increasingly frustrated by the *shilly shallying* of both MacDonald and Baldwin regarding rearmament, cynically suspecting that their prevarication was perhaps deliberately intended to enable both to announce, *with a sigh of relief 'Now it is too late to do anything'*. The three service departments were in a lamentable state particularly the *hopeless* Air Ministry led by *poor Charlie Londonderry* the Air Minister who *means well but he never does himself justice*, a feeling which no doubt contributed to Londonderry's dismissal the following month. The country was hardly better served by the complacency of Chief of the Air Staff Edward Ellington who *makes us all despair*, opined Chamberlain.[26] Chamberlain was glad, however, that, despite Churchill's appointment to the newly-formed Air Defence Research Committee, his first taste of government since 1929, he still remained outside the Cabinet. *He is in the usual excited condition that comes on him when he smells war*, observed Chamberlain, *and if he were in the Cabinet we should be spending all our time in holding him down instead of getting on with business.*[27]

By the spring of 1936 Chamberlain was *pretty satisfied that if we can keep out of war for a few years we shall have an air force of such striking power that no one will care to run risks with it.*[28] The second White Paper, *Statement Relating to Defence* published on 3 March 1936, which outlined a programme to build two new battleships and an aircraft carrier, increasing the number of cruisers from 50 to 70, creating four new infantry battalions, augmentation of territorial and coastal defence and an increase in the frontline strength of the Royal Air Force from 1,500 to 1,750 first-line planes, was largely Chamberlain's work.[29] Chamberlain was also an effusive champion of the fighter plane and, although still in

The RAF's first monoplane fighter, and the first to fly at more than 300mph, the Hawker Hurricane entered squadron service in December 1937. Although less famous than the Spitfire, the Hurricane actually bore the major part in the fighting in the Battle of Britain, equipping 32 squadrons, and between 2 August and 31 October 1940 a daily average of 1,326 Hurricanes saw action as opposed to 957 Spitfires. By 1945, 14,533 Hurricanes in three marks had been built, seeing service in all theatres of the war, including on the Eastern Front where 2,952 aircraft were supplied to the Soviet Union.

its infancy – the first Hawker Hurricane prototypes rolled off the production line towards the end of 1935 – Chamberlain was impressed by the *astonishing ingenuity and inventiveness* with which rearmament was being approached, believing by the summer of 1936 that fresh researches, *for the first time seem to open up gleams of hope in the direction of air defence*, though this optimism belied serious deficiencies in the capability of Britain's bomber force which in 1938 remained inferior to that of Germany.[30]

Rearmament remained an unpopular proposition until at least 1938. It was vociferously opposed by a large proportion of the Labour movement and internationally by the League of Nations who, on 27 June 1935, announced the results of its 'peace ballot' in which some 11.5 million people had taken part. Of those who expressed a clear preference, 85 per cent of respondents favoured the abolition of military aircraft and 94 per cent wanted to punish aggressor nations with collective economic sanctions rather than punitive military action. Unmoved by public opinion Chamberlain advocated that the government *should take the bold course of actually appealing to the country on a defence programme*. Ever attuned to the prevailing climate of opinion, Baldwin publicly repudiated such an idea, as did Chamberlain, though the latter confided to his diary that German expenditure and industrial organisation was such that the Nazi desire for territorial expansion was unlikely to be sated and thus, *we must hurry our own rearmament and in the course of the next 4 or 5 years we shall probably have to spend an extra £120 millions in doing so*. Such plans, which would necessitate an unpopular rise in tax to offset inflation, were not, deemed *sufficiently advanced* to be shared with the electorate as a result of which both Chamberlain and Baldwin deliberately played down future commitments to vastly increased defence expenditure during the general election campaign of

November 1935.[31] As a result in February 1936 the services' report to the Cabinet committee granted the navy as many warships as it could procure for the protection of British trade, pledged to meet the needs of the RAF but deferred almost all of the recommendations of the army, in effect ruling out its use as a continental expeditionary force, a lessening in its capabilities which neither Alfred Duff Cooper, Secretary for War or Sir Thomas Inskip, the newly Minister for the Co-ordination of Defence succeeded in reversing, a lacuna that was not corrected until 1939. Chamberlain was also the architect of the financial framework, which strictly limited government interference with civilian production, particularly the transfer of skilled workers to the production of armaments, lest it adversely affected Britain's export trade or jeopardise Britain's returning prosperity. For Chamberlain, the subordination of rearmament to the financial necessity of balancing the books and restoring a strong economy – the *fourth arm of defence* – meant that Chamberlain, 'virtually dictated the rearmament plan that Cabinet eventually approved'.[32]

On 11 February 1937 Chamberlain announced to the House his intention to obtain authority to borrow a further £400 million for rearmament over the next five years. This was followed five days later by the third White Paper, *Statement Relating to Defence*, which proposed that anything short of a total expenditure of £1,500 million on defence over the next five years would be *imprudent* though both Chamberlain and the Treasury did their best to curtail any profligate spending by the army in particular, a process eased by the departure of Duff Cooper and his replacement by the pliant Leslie Hore-Belisha. In April 1937 as part of his final budget as Chancellor Chamberlain unveiled the National Defence Contribution (NDC), a graduated tax on business profits attributable to rearmament. It was massively unpopular and occasioned *violent and premature abuse* from his own party, business and the city though Chamberlain rated it to be *the bravest thing I have ever done since I was in public life.* Chamberlain also saw the NDC as a public relations exercise aimed at silencing his more voluble critics who were demanding rearmament by proving *that there are limits to the amount of money at their disposal* for rearmament.[33] Although Chamberlain continued to defend the measure it was replaced by his successor in June with a 5 per cent tax on business profits.

Yet even while Chamberlain grappled with the fiscal complexities of rearmament, his role as Chancellor demanded he continue to undertake a multitude of other tasks including championing the unemployment assistance board against a sustained media assault on his position by Lloyd George and his 'New Deal' proposals, brokering a reconciliation with Lord Beaverbrook, formulated a new policy for the Colonial Office, the India Bill, the protection of British interests in China and the Special Areas (Amendment) Bill, which Chamberlain regarded as a great personal triumph not least because it caused a great deal of discomfiture for Lloyd George who had steadfastly opposed the measure and accused Chamberlain of a lack of sympathy with those it was designed to aid. Indeed, despite the increasingly desperate situation pertaining to rearmament Chamberlain

If only it wasn't for Germany we should be having such a wonderful time just now.
CHAMBERLAIN

was in little doubt that the domestic aspect of the administration was a success. *If only it wasn't for Germany we should be having such a wonderful time just now*, he lamented.[34]

By the mid-1930s Chamberlain's close and mutually beneficial working relationship with Baldwin, temperamentally his polar opposite, was nearing its end. Chamberlain had always harboured a grudging admiration for Baldwin's ability to get away with skating *over or around points of controversy* but since 1935 he had been increasingly convinced that Baldwin needed to resign.[35] Broaching the subject was no easy matter, however. Having advised Baldwin that the St Georges Westminster by-election in March 1931 might have a deleterious effect upon his successor, Chamberlain was met with the retort: 'I don't give a damn about my successor, Neville.'[36] Four years later in May 1935 Baldwin confided to Chamberlain his desire to remain in office until he was 70 (i.e. 3 August 1937), though Chamberlain doubted he would last that long.[37] He was not unaware, however, that Baldwin was an immensely influential figure throughout the country. *I am bound to recognise*, he wrote to his sister, *that if I supply the policy and the drive S.B. does also supply something that is perhaps even more valuable in retaining the floating vote.*[38] Despite his frustration with Baldwin's lacklustre leadership Chamberlain was in no hurry to challenge him. Continuing as Chancellor of the Exchequer after the 1935 general election and pondered the possibility of his own retirement, Chamberlain was resigned to the fact that Baldwin would stay the course by which time, *I shall be 70 and shant care much I daresay for the strenuous life of leader even if some one else hasn't overtaken me before then.*[39] Baldwin's deterioration, probably the result of a nervous breakdown, continued throughout 1936 and he became, in Chamberlain's view, *more and more disinclined to make any sustained effort* meaning that Chamberlain, although frustrated *to have a leader who gives no lead in this particularly trying time*, was essentially the *de facto* head of government.[40] Following Baldwin's recuperation in France in August 1936 Chamberlain finally pinned him down on the question of the succession. *He would have been quite capable of saying nothing about it and leaving it to the press to run alternative candidates*, Chamberlain sighed.[41]

The final days of Baldwin's premiership were overshadowed

by the abdication crisis in which King Edward VIII's amorous affair with an American divorcee precipitated a major constitutional crisis, threatening the foundations of the British monarchy. Although Baldwin deftly dealt with the crisis Chamberlain was exasperated by what he perceived to be his lack of urgency believing that it was he who had *prodded* Baldwin to warn the King of the consequences of his actions. Appalled by Baldwin's vacillation Chamberlain secretly made the necessary enquiries as to the King's powers, the limitations of the government's powers and the procedures that would be necessary in a variety of scenarios and even drafted a number of communiqués which he felt might be necessary before obtaining the backing of a number of colleagues for his proposals. Only then did he inform Baldwin.[42] On the morning of 10 December 1936 the 'long trial' was over. King Edward VIII signed a Deed of Abdication. Chamberlain heaved *a big sigh of relief* tempered by the fear that the marriage *must end speedily in disillusionment and disgust* largely due to the character of Wallis Simpson herself whom Chamberlain believed was *a thoroughly selfish & heartless adventuress*. Baldwin meanwhile *reaped a rich harvest of credit*, some of which Chamberlain conceded he deserved, which carried him *to the highest pinnacle of his career*.[43] Baldwin determined to hang on until the Coronation of King George VI in May 1937 in order to 'see *this* young man through'.[44] True to his word Baldwin resigned shortly afterwards. 'No Prime Minister has ever chosen a better moment to bow himself out,' observed the Conservative historian Lord Blake approvingly.[45] Right until the final moment Chamberlain, whilst professing not to care, inevitably reflected on his father and half-brother's failure to achieve the highest office, wondered *whether Fate has some dark secret in store to carry out her ironies to the end*.[46] It did not. Nominated by Churchill and Lord Derby, Chamberlain became Prime Minister on 28 May 1937.

Part Two

THE LEADERSHIP

Chapter 4: Prime Minister

When Chamberlain was summoned to Buckingham Palace on 28 May 1937 his normally unflappable persona was slightly ruffled by his confusion as to whether the phrase to 'kiss hands' with the King ought to be *interpreted literally*. Fortunately the King did not offer his hand when appointing Chamberlain Prime Minister and, as Chamberlain made no effort to seize it, a potentially embarrassing situation was averted.[1] That afternoon, having seen the King, Chamberlain sent Buckingham Palace the list of his Cabinet 'down to the last button'. Chamberlain's ministers, mostly veterans of the National Government, were sworn in that evening.[2] Reflecting on his succession to the highest office in the land, a post denied to both his father and his half-brother, Chamberlain recorded his bemusement that, *it has come to me without my raising a finger to obtain it, because there is no one else and perhaps because I have not made enemies by looking after myself rather than the common cause.*[3]

As was to be expected from a man as punctilious as Chamberlain, one of his first acts was to inform all his legislating ministers that he required a two-year programme from them ready for the autumn when he would collate and prioritise their position in the two-year provisional plan for action he was drafting. Although at 68 Chamberlain was already at an age when most men have retired, one of the most extraordinary things about him, noted Lord Templewood, was his 'inexhaustible resiliency' despite being periodically visited by painful attacks of gout that frequently left him bedridden with his right foot encased in a specially-made boot. Yet Chamberlain doggedly refused to let his ailments distract him from matters of state.[4] Indeed, despite one particularly painful attack just after he assumed office, Chamberlain remained optimistic that *I may have long enough to leave my mark behind me as P.M.*[5] Chamberlain envisaged his premiership as the crowning glory on his reputation as a domestic reformer, having little idea that his political epitaph was soon to be disfigured by his handling of international affairs.

Following his elevation to the premiership Chamberlain's autocratic traits of leadership were exacerbated as he quickly assumed what Lord Swinton lamented as 'the pretensions of the Presidential system of one-man government'.[6] Chamberlain's style of government is worthy of further examination for it underpins his personal responsibility for the spectacular failure of British foreign policy. Chamberlain did not rush to judgement, ruminating and cogitating for hours on matters of state in private before announcing his verdict. As Lord Simon noted, there were no 'sudden inspirations or sensational shortcuts' just a 'steely persistence' that the 'hard labour of his own brains' could solve any problem no matter what its magnitude.[7] Chamberlain's close confidant Sir Horace Wilson refuted the idea that Chamberlain ignored his Cabinet whilst formulating policy. Chamberlain 'was always ready to consider carefully views and arguments put before him and he took time before making up his mind what course to follow,' noted Wilson. However, 'when that course was settled he did not wonder whether it was right and whether it would have been better to decide to try something else'.[8] The Liberal leader Herbert Samuel was perhaps nearer the mark, however, in his observation that although Chamberlain 'was always willing to listen to arguments with a friendly spirit' he did do with 'a closed mind'.[9] It was with this in mind that the journalist Ian Colvin was convinced that Chamberlain's final consultation with 'the inner Cabinet' was only entertained in order to fortify his resolve in a decision already reached.[10]

Once convinced that he had complete mastery over his arguments, Chamberlain's method was to wear his opponents down intellectually, remorselessly subjecting them to *the same course of reasoning as I have followed myself*.[11] Chamberlain saw no reason why the same rationale was not applicable when dealing with the dictators. The idea that this was not possible he greeted with 'sustained astonishment'.[12] With no time for introspective post-mortem, Chamberlain's sense of infallibility, born from his solitary experiences as a young man on Andros where there had been 'no one else to judge', meant that he was not to be distracted by 'the details of his journey'.[13] Indeed, his 'growing vanity and self-righteousness' reinforced Chamberlain's imperviousness to criticism or deviation once this ultimate destination was recognised.[14] As he recorded following a particularly rough ride in the House of Commons during a debate on Spain in June 1938: *I think what enables me to come through such an ordeal successfully is that fact that I am completely convinced that the course I am taking is right and therefore cannot be influenced by the attacks of my critics*.[15] Chamberlain joked about the venom he endured, particularly from the Labour movement when considering a recent article about his speeches, which observed that he had been the subject of more bitter hostility than any Prime Minister since 1919. *I am inclined to fancy that this is true*, noted Chamberlain, *although I cannot understand why, because I am the most reasonable of men and I never object to opposition so long as I can have my own way*.[16] Although Chamberlain claimed not to let such criticism disturb his peace of mind, occasionally he did find the *poison gas* of the House of Commons oppressively dispiriting and turned for solace to the many letters expressing *heartfelt relief and gratitude* that poured into Number 10.[17] Their sympathy was wasted, however, *as I do not trouble over criticisms which do not affect my judgement of what is right*, Chamberlain wrote,

like William Pitt (1708–78) 'I know that I can save this country and I do not believe that anyone else can'.[18] It would certainly appear that Chamberlain's overweening egotism blinded him to what was to become increasingly obvious to even the most hardened appeaser like Lord Halifax: that Hitler was not someone with whom one could treat.

It is often taken for granted that the disastrous failure of Chamberlain's policy of appeasement arose from a combination of these personal traits and his ignorance of foreign affairs. It would be a tremendous indictment against Chamberlain were it true, particularly if he ignored expert views to the contrary, a point which will be addressed in the following chapter. Chamberlain's supposed ignorance of foreign affairs was widely muted at the time. 'An earnest and opinionated provincial was bound to err if he plunged into diplomacy,' Foreign Office mandarin Sir Robert Vansittart recorded with ducal disdain.[19] Such dismal impressions are reinforced by the undue prominence given by historians to an incident captured in Anthony Eden's autobiography in which Austen Chamberlain gently admonished his younger half-brother, 'Neville, you must remember you don't know anything about foreign affairs.'[20] Yet if this is how Eden recorded his views for posterity they were certainly not his views contemporaneously. Eden's devoted political secretary O C Harvey recorded his master's delight at the prospect of a more hands-on premier, noting that Eden and Chamberlain 'fully shared' each other's views. 'There nothing really to divide them,' observed Harvey.[21] Chamberlain also confided in Leslie Hore-Belisha, however, that, 'he intended to take a new line' with regards to foreign policy though this radical departure failed to materialise.[22] After the lethargy of Baldwin's stewardship the prospect that Chamberlain would take a 'personal' interest in foreign affairs was warmly greeted by the majority of Conservative parliamentarians.[23] Eden was oblivious, at least initially, to the fact that Chamberlain meant to be his own Foreign Minister.

Chamberlain was not, however, an international ignoramus. Since his earliest days as a Birmingham businessman he had taken a keen interest in foreign affairs, recognising well before 1914 that Germany was not to be bound by ententes and treaties. Indeed, given the complexities of the world crisis after 1929 Chamberlain, as Chancellor of the Exchequer, was intimately involved in foreign affairs. As David Dutton observes, it was Chamberlain rather than the Foreign Secretary who headed the British delegation to Lausanne in 1932 to resolve the question of reparations, though their cessation came too late to save Bruning's government.[24] Indeed it was probably his belief that the Foreign Secretary was the *weak point* in the government that convinced Chamberlain that he needed to be more personally involved in the direction of foreign policy.[25] Although Chamberlain never coveted the position of Foreign Secretary himself, perhaps because he felt uncomfortable with the trappings of the office – *I should hate the journeys to Geneva and above all I should loathe and detest the social ceremonies* – senior figures in the Conservative Party including Baldwin, Churchill, the Chief Whip David Margesson, not to mention Ramsay MacDonald, had all periodically considered Chamberlain worthy of the post.[26] It is therefore rather hard to credit the disastrous diplomacy of the 1930s to Chamberlain's ignorance of foreign affairs but rather that his absolute certitude in the righteousness of his own decisions precluded the consideration of alternative courses of action.

Chamberlain was sympathetic towards Hitler's early efforts to revise the inequitable Treaty of Versailles and no doubt sympathised with Germany's imperial urges. He was keen to resolve its contentious clauses, which would enable him to concentrate on domestic issues. *They want much the same thing for the Sudeten Deutsch as we did for the Uitlanders in the Transvaal,* Chamberlain once observed. It is often forgotten that many politicians of his generation saw the Sudeten Deutsch as German and so saw no reason why Germany should not absorb them, thus righting another wrong of the Versailles settlement.[27] Indeed, it was the method rather than the aim of Hitler's expansionist foreign policy to which Chamberlain objected. Although his understanding of Nazism's dynamics was rudimentary, Germany's blatant rearmament and flagrant disregard for the disarmament conference was coupled in Chamberlain's mind with the brutal assassination of the Austrian Chancellor Dollfuss which *makes me hate Nazism and all its works with a greater loathing than ever.*[28] Likewise, although Chamberlain's personal letters occasionally reverberated with a certain parlour anti-Semitism – *no doubt Jews aren't a lovable people; I don't care for them myself* – he had no sympathy with the Nazis' persecution of the Jews, though neither did it cause him any undue cause for concern.[29] Indeed, fundamentally Chamberlain felt the internal politics of Germany were its own concern.

Although Chamberlain's name will in all probability forever be associated with the policy of 'appeasement', he was not the progenitor of the idea. This honour belongs to the Foreign Office itself which initiated it in 1931 as a initiative through which peace could be restored to Europe through the removal of the sources of friction arising from the Treaty of Versailles, issues such as the demilitarisation of the Rhineland, arms limitation and restrictions on German exports and, eventually, the restoration of her colonies which was to become an increasingly fraught question. British foreign policy had followed a similar theme since the 19th century in an effort to avoid imperial overstretch. This made sound diplomatic sense for a small island. It was only in 1937 when Chamberlain became Prime Minister that appeasement underwent the profound shift from being a policy of diplomatic revision to one of capitulation. Chamberlain recognised that Germany was *the bully of Europe* and was determined to make its pacification the epicentre of his foreign policy, redressing its grievances whilst also attending to those of Italy and in doing so drive a wedge between Hitler and Mussolini.[30] And then there was Japan to contend with, which was menacing British interests in the Far East. For Chamberlain appeasement representing a 'double policy' coupling the deterrence of rearmament, which as Chancellor of the Exchequer he had put his personal seal upon, with Anglo-German and Anglo-Italian *rapprochement*. Chamberlain saw no contradiction between these two goals, viewing appeasement as the only way forward. Yet Chamberlain's excessively emollient brand of appeasement bent over backwards to placate the *bully* by sacrificing weaker nations for Britain's own protection. It was hardly creditable morally and not exactly what the Foreign Office had in mind when it originally considered the question of restoring the balance of power in Europe. Chamberlain, however, was contemptuous of any other initiatives aimed at collective security. Much of this wrath in this respect was directed towards the domestic Labour movement and internationally towards the League of Nations, which he believed

The Special Relationship

'On the evening of January 11, 1938, Mr. Sumner Welles, the American Under-Secretary of State, called upon the British Ambassador in Washington. He was the bearer of a secret and confidential message from President Roosevelt to Mr. Chamberlain. The President was deeply anxious at the deterioration of the international situation, and proposed to take the initiative by inviting the representatives of certain Governments to Washington to discuss the underlying causes of present difficulties. Before taking this step however he wished to consult the British Government on their view of such a plan, and stipulated that other Government should be informed either of the nature or the existence of such a proposal. He asked that not later than January 17 he should be given a reply to his message, and intimated that only if his suggestion met with "the cordial approval and whole-hearted support of His Majesty's Government" would he then approach the Governments of France, Germany and Italy. Here was a formidable and measureless step.

... Mr. Chamberlain's reply was to the effect that he appreciated the confidence of President Roosevelt in consulting him ... but he wished to explain the position of his own efforts to reach agreement with Germany and Italy, particularly in the case of the latter. "His Majesty's Government would be prepared, for their part, if possible with the authority of the League of Nations, to recognise *de jure* the Italian occupation of Abyssinia, if they found that the Italian Government on their side were ready to give evidence of their desire to contribute to the restoration of confidence and friendly relations." ... The President's letter reached London on the morning of January 18. In it he agreed to postpone making his proposal in view of the fact that the British Government were contemplating direct negotiations, but he added that he was gravely concerned at the suggestion that His Majesty's Government might accord recognition to the Italian position in Abyssinia. He thought that this would have a most harmful effect upon Japanese policy in the Far East and upon American public opinion.' [Winston Churchill, *The Second World War,* Vol I (Cassell & Co, London: 1948) pp 196f.]

was incapable of providing collective security; it attracted only Liberals and cranks and was thus incapable of achieving its goals.[31] Britain, however, had blocked French attempts in 1934 to establish an 'Eastern Locarno', which, with the backing of a Franco-Soviet guarantee, would provide collective security for Eastern Europe. Britain undermined the deal by adopting the position of 'benevolent wellwishers' and the idea collapsed completely when both Poland and Germany refused to ratify it.

Italy was central to appeasement. Chamberlain famously regarded sanctions against Italy as *the very midsummer of madness* (later conceding that this remark was *a blazing indiscretion*) and took the lead in bringing them to an end.[32] Following Mussolini's invasion of Abyssinia in 1935 the Foreign Secretary Samuel Hoare was forced to resign following the public outcry which accompanied revelations in the press of the terms of the Hoare-Laval pact whereby Britain and France had covertly attempted to hand Mussolini large tracts of Abyssinia.[33] Hoare was replaced in December 1935 by the suave Anthony Eden, whose tenure as Foreign Secretary was almost immediately complicated by the outbreak of the Spanish Civil War in July 1936. This brought him into conflict with Chamberlain, then Chancellor of the Exchequer, whose backing of the Non-Intervention Pact was designed to keep Britain from being drawn into the conflict by refusing to recognise belligerent rights on either side until Franco's fascist-backed insurgency won out in March 1939. This was another reason Chamberlain was loathed by the Labour

As Ch. Of Ex. I could hardly have moved a pebble, now I have only to raise a finger & the whole face of Europe is changed!

CHAMBERLAIN

movement. *I believe any other course would have got us into very serious trouble*, observed an unrepentant Chamberlain, *but once again I ask myself what would have happened if I had not been there. I doubt if anyone realizes or will ever realize how many scrapes I have saved this and the last Government from.*[34]

Eden and Chamberlain were in complete agreement that Germany represented the greatest danger to the European balance of power. *If only we could get on terms with the Germans I would not care a rap for Musso*, Chamberlain noted in July 1937.[35] Nevertheless Mussolini remained a fly in the ointment throughout 1937 primarily due to his demand that Britain grant his conquest of Abyssinia *de jure* recognition. Chamberlain was keen to assent to this *as part of a great scheme of reconciliation*, which would win the British government greater room for manoeuvre when dealing with both Germany and Japan.[36] Chamberlain was well aware that his personal meetings on the subject with Count Dino Grandi, the Italian Ambassador in London, had wounded Eden's vanity and so kept secret his personal letters to Mussolini.[37] The temptation to interfere in foreign affairs was too much for Chamberlain. He derived a wonderful sense of power from his meetings with Grandi. *As Ch. Of Ex. I could hardly have moved a pebble*, enthused Chamberlain, *now I have only to raise a finger & the whole face of Europe is changed!*[38] Chamberlain believed the restoration of Anglo-Italian relations, which had deteriorated following Mussolini's invasion of Abyssinia and declined further as a result of his intervention in the Spanish Civil War, represented *a very important step forward towards European appeasement* and side-stepped objections from the Foreign Office to mollify the dictator.[39] This emollient approach frequently led Chamberlain to rewrite Foreign Office dispatches, castigating them for having *no imagination & no courage*. Not that the servile Eden objected. *A. E. is awfully good in accepting my suggestions without grumbling*, noted Chamberlain approvingly.[40]

Chamberlain was irritated by Foreign Office's *frigid* approach to world affairs, however, becoming increasingly convinced that a *fresh start* was necessary if the pursuit of a general settlement was to become realisable.[41] Matters reached a climax on 3 October 1937 when Lord Halifax, as master of the foxhounds, received an invite from Prince Lowenstein, president of the German Hunting Association and the editor of *Field*, to attend an international sporting exhibition in Berlin enabling him to meet senior dignitaries in the process. Despite its difficulties Chamberlain viewed the visit as *a great success* and an essential precursor to convincing Hitler of British sincerity and an opportunity to ascertain his real objectives. Hitler intimated to Halifax that union with Austria was 'imperative'. Halifax replied that England favoured any solution provided 'that it be not based on force, and that applied to Austria'. Hitler interpreted this, not unsurprisingly, as tacit approval of his action.[42] Halifax's report contributed to Chamberlain's exceedingly naïve view of German intentions, bolstering his belief that Hitler did not want war, only to unite with Austria, and *to dominate Eastern Europe* whilst seeking the resolution of the *Sudentendeutsche* and regain former colonial possessions in Togoland and Cameroon. Chamberlain hoped to induce Hitler to return to the League of Nations if it were shorn of its (ineffective) compulsory powers. Although Hitler was apparently non-committal about disarmament, *he did declare himself in favour of the abolition of bombing aeroplanes*, which Chamberlain regarded as especially significant. Although there were inevitable difficulties attached to each point Chamberlain regarded them as *a fair basis of discussion*. All of this seemed entirely reasonable to Chamberlain. As he wrote to his sister *I don't see why we shouldn't say to Germany Give us satisfactory assurances that you wont use force to deal with the Austrian & Czecho-Slovakians & we will give you similar assurances that we wont use force to prevent the changes you want if you can get them by peaceful means.*[43]

Relations between Eden and Chamberlain were becoming increasingly strained, however, as Chamberlain recording his fear that *at bottom he is really against making terms with the dictators*.[44] Halifax's Berlin visit polarised matters. Both Eden and the fiercely anti-German Foreign Office mandarin Sir Robert Vansittart had opposed it. From thereon Chamberlain was only waiting the opportunity to stir the Foreign Office up *with a long pole*.[45] Chamberlain was also increasingly disturbed by Eden's bellicosity, which he saw as part and parcel of a wider Foreign Office tendency to react to the detail of international affairs at the expense of wider diplomatic aims which he believed gave the dictators common cause. It took Chamberlain just three days to have Vansittart 'kicked upstairs' to the largely powerless post of Chief Diplomatic Advisor. Chamberlain replaced him with Sir Alexander Cadogan, 'a slow sane man', whose appointment was calculated to reduce international friction and remove a baleful influence upon Eden, who was equally glad to be rid of Vansittart.[46] Eden was increasingly incensed, however, by Chamberlain's continued reliance on back-door diplomacy. Without consulting Eden, Chamberlain had dispatched Lady Ivy Chamberlain, his half-brother's widow, to Rome in December 1937 to discuss the

Lord Halifax (1881–1959) had been Viceroy of India (as Lord Irwin) from 1926 to 1931, where he negotiated an agreement with Gandhi to suspend the civil disobedience campaign, which unfortunately proved short-lived. After replacing Eden as Foreign Secretary in 1938, he bore much of the later blame for appeasement and the mishandling of the 'Phoney War'. Widely tipped to succeed Chamberlain in 1940, he ruled himself out as he was in the Lords and unacceptable to Labour, and thus unable to form a truly national government. Churchill made him ambassador to the USA a few months later.

resumption of Anglo-Italian talks. Ball too opened his own covert channels with Italian officials in London designed to circumvent the Foreign Office. Eden was outraged and Chamberlain determined *that Anthony must yield or go*. Eden went on 18 February, much to Chamberlain's satisfaction.[47] His resignation made little impact, not least because he refrained from attacking Chamberlain who retained the confidence of both the House of Commons and the party, thanks partly to an effective campaign orchestrated by Ball.[48] Lord Halifax replaced Eden, a sign of Chamberlain's intention to mould foreign policy to his own image.

Eden had also been deeply critical of the way Chamberlain had dismissed the idea of Anglo-American co-operation as a counterweight to Italy's decision to join Germany and Japan as signatories to the Anti-Comintern Pact in November 1937.[49] The failure of sanctions against Italy made Chamberlain unwilling to acquiesce to the idea implicit in President Roosevelt's 'quarantine' speech on 5 October 1937 which exhorted sanctions against the Japanese lest such a move provoke a conflagration in the Far East which in turn could easily be exploited by the dictators to force Britain's (militarily unprepared) hand in Europe. Nor was Chamberlain willing to assent to the terms of Roosevelt's secret telegram on 8 January 1938 proposing a world conference to limit the arms race in return for equal access to raw materials, which he hoped would restore the international order. Chamberlain had long been irritated by America's *calm assumption* that Britain had *nothing else to do but serve American interests: to think of British interests is to shatter American confidence in our good faith*.[50] Backed by his close advisor Sir Horace Wilson who believed the proposals 'woolly rubbish', Chamberlain succeeded, after *much time and some very uncomfortable moments*, in batting the President's proposal into the long grass, by stating that they might *cut across* his efforts to restore relations with Mussolini, much to Eden's chagrin.[51]

The restoration of Germany's former colonies, confiscated by the Treaty of Versailles, loomed large towards the end of 1937 as a precursor to a general settlement in Europe. Hitler was overwhelmingly hostile to the idea as presented to him by Sir Neville Henderson, the egregious British Ambassador in Berlin who, unusually, regarded himself as Chamberlain's personal envoy. The issue was completely overshadowed only days later on 9 March 1938 by Hitler's annexation of Austria. Chamberlain was flabbergasted. Nevertheless it confirmed his opinion that he had been right not to publish Roosevelt's proposal, as Eden had urged him to, because it would have made Britain *the laughing stock of the world*.[52] Chamberlain had just met with von Ribbentrop to discuss greater Anglo-German understanding when news of the *Anschluss* reached him. He immediately recalled the former champagne salesman for a second meeting, which left Chamberlain *overcome by a feeling of helplessness*. Ribbentrop simply failed to comprehend the British government's basic objection to *German methods*. The *Anschluss* indicated to Chamberlain that the idea of collective security was obsolete unless Britain could show Germany it had the material muscle to enforce its demands. Faced with such a situation Chamberlain even began contemplating a system of alliances, though pointedly not on the model of the League of Nations that would *require meetings at Geneva and resolutions by dozens of small nations who have no responsibilities*.[53] In the days following the *Anschluss* Chamberlain revived ideas for a continental alliance with Halifax, the chiefs of staff and the Foreign Office. The attraction of such a scheme soon vanished. Chamberlain's appraisal of the situation was that there was nothing that either Britain or France could do to save Czechoslovakia if Germany chose to invade, a bleak assessment which led him to abandon, *any idea of giving guarantees to Czecho-Slovakia or to France in connection with her obligations to that country.*[54] Refusing to cry over *spilt milk*, Chamberlain continued to entertain the idea of persuading Hitler to enter into a joint guarantee of Czechoslovakian independence. *I believe the Germans might listen*, he wrote optimistically, particularly as Anglo-Italian relations were temporarily showing signs of improvement, though he soon abandoned the idea.[55]

On 28 March Chamberlain and Halifax both made pronouncements to the House of Commons which, whilst not specifically mentioning Czechoslovakia, cautioned that if war broke out 'it would be quite impossible to say where it might end and what Governments might become involved'. Chamberlain also announced major increases in rearmament expenditure. Despite the precarious international situation Chamberlain felt *there can be no question that I have got the confidence of our people as S.B. never had it.*[56] The clouds appeared to clear on 16 April 1938 when the Anglo-Italian agreement was signed, recognising Mussolini's conquest of Abyssinia in return for the withdrawal of 'volunteers' from Spain, though this did not actually come into force until 16 November. Chamberlain oversaw the publication of the mutual exchange of letters between himself and Mussolini personally redrafting the original Foreign Office response that *would have frozen a Polar Bear!*[57] To Chamberlain's mind the *Anschluss* gave the Rome-Berlin Axis *a nasty jar*, the results of which could be seen in Mussolini's lukewarm response to Hitler's tour of Italy at the beginning of May, designed to induce Italian support for his annexation of Czechoslovakia. Chamberlain therefore set great store in the conclusion of the Anglo-Italian agreement, which he hoped would aid British foreign policy in Central and Eastern Europe where, *we may hope for a good deal of quiet hope from Italy*.[58]

He was less optimistic about the prospect of France as an ally, however. Whilst Chamberlain found the Prime Minister Daladier *simple and straightforward*, he lamented that the *French are not very fortunate in their Foreign Secretaries*.[59] Instead of blaming Nazi imperialism for the European crisis, Chamberlain believed Britain had been brought to this impasse by the hubris of the French who had recklessly guaranteed Czechoslovakia's sovereignty without the strength to honour their commitment. Unable to renege on this commitment for reasons of national prestige the French, believed Chamberlain, were perfidiously seeking to draw the British into the frame to assuage their own guilty conscience. At the same time, however, Britain could not countenance the destruction of France. Chamberlain's fears were hardly allayed by Earl Winterton who, on 12 May, put in a less-than-competent defence of British defence policy, leading him to be heckled throughout by Churchill, Attlee and others. It was, noted Chamberlain, *the worst day in the House ... that I have experienced since I became P.M.*[60] As a result Chamberlain was forced to sack his friend and replace him with Kingsley Wood as Air Minister.

Chapter 5: Munich

Throughout May 1938 Germany continued to stalk the Czech border, which, on the 19th, occasioned the mobilisation of Czech reservists. Chamberlain believed that British warnings had been instrumental in forestalling a coup as well as underlining to him *how utterly untrustworthy and dishonest the German Government is and it illuminates the difficulties in the way of the peacemaker.*[1] It was an important observation and one which would have born Chamberlain in good stead had he remembered it a few months later. Instead he entertained the fantasy that his position on the Continent *is one of great influence.*[2] On 18 July Captain Fritz Wiedemann visited Britain to reiterate Hitler's desire for continued Anglo-German friendship and to reassure Chamberlain that Germany 'was planning no resort to force' over the Sudeten question and might, barring a serious, unforeseen incident, consent to give a formal promise to this effect, 'limited to a definite period'. The international situation continued to decline, however, and on 3 August the British government learned that Hitler was planning a partial test mobilisation, the same day that Viscount Walter Runciman was dispatched to Czechoslovakia to act as 'conciliator and mediator' between Germany and Czechoslovakia regarding the 'Sudeten question'.

On 11 August Hitler was warned that, 'a situation might rapidly arise in which ... the peace of every one of the Great

The Irish Ports

'The reader is now invited to move westward to the Emerald Isle. "It's a long way to Tipperary", but a visit there is sometimes irresistible. In the interval between Hitler's seizure of Austria and his unfolding design upon Czechoslovakia we must turn to a wholly different kind of misfortune which befell us.

Since the beginning of 1938 there had been negotiations between the British Government and that of Mr. de Valera in Southern Ireland, and on April 25 an agreement was signed whereby among other matters Great Britain renounced all rights to occupy for naval purposes the two Southern Irish ports of Queenstown and Berehaven, and the base in Lough Swilly. The two Southern ports were a vital feature in the naval defence of our food supply... .

It was incredible to me that the Chiefs of Staff should have agreed to throw away this major security, and to the last moment I thought that at least we had safeguarded our right to occupy these Irish ports in the event of war. However, Mr. de Valera announced in the Dail that no conditions of any kind were attached to the cession. I was later assured that Mr. de Valera was surprised at the readiness with which the British Government had deferred to his request. He had included it in his proposals as a bargaining-counter which could be dispensed with when other points were satisfactorily settled.

... The whole Conservative Party, except the handful of Ulster members, supported the Prime Minister, and of course a step like this was meat and drink to the Labour and Liberal Opposition. I was therefore almost entirely alone when on May 5 I rose to make my protest. I was listened to with a patient air of scepticism. There was even a kind of sympathetic wonder that anyone of my standing should attempt to plead so hopeless a case. I never saw the House of Commons more completely misled. It was but fifteen months to the declaration of war. The members were to feel very differently about it when our existence hung in the balance during the Battle of the Atlantic. [Winston Churchill, *The Second World War*, Vol I (Cassell & Co, London: 1948) pp 215f.]

Powers of Europe might be endangered.' And Hitler did everything he could to endanger the peace of Europe, instructing Konrad Henlein's Sudeten Germans to continue demanding autonomy within Czechoslovakia. An emergency meeting of the British Cabinet on 30 August refused to issue an ultimatum to Hitler and instead opted to put pressure on the Czechs to meet Henlein's demands. After six days of agonising deliberation the Czech President Eduard Beneš finally acquiesced. Henlein was astonished. He had not expected Beneš to agree. Indeed in doing so he had completely undermined Hitler's pretext for war. Hitler was set on war, however. Even before Beneš's acquiescence Karl Frank, Henlein's right-hand man, was ordered to instigate provocative 'incidents', an order reiterated the day before Beneš's agreement, leaving Frank in no doubt that the '*Führer* is determined on war.' Despite this Henlein deceived his British contact that Hitler continued to favour a peaceful solution, which further fuelled the hopes of the appeasers.[3]

Chamberlain's Minister of Defence, the ebullient *bon viveur* Duff Cooper, favoured issuing Hitler with an unambiguous warning that the invasion of Czechoslovakia would result in a general European war, an idea that cut little ice with either Lord Halifax or Chamberlain who believed bellicosity would only raise Hitler's ire and therefore increase the likelihood of war. Indeed, Chamberlain believed that to cajole and threaten Germany without having the material backing to make good its threats would make Britain look absurd. Chamberlain's mode of thinking was *fortified* by his reading of Professor Arthur Temperly's *The Foreign Policy of Canning* (1925), which made a deep impression upon him when he read it just prior to the Munich crisis. *Again and again Canning lays it down that you should never menace unless you are in a position to carry out your threats*, he recorded for the benefit of his sister.[4] Whilst waiting for Hitler's speech to the Nazi faithful at Nuremberg on 6 September 1938 Chamberlain had asked himself, *is it not positively horrible to think that the fate of hundreds of millions depends on one man and he is half mad*. Soon afterwards he conceived of 'Plan Z' – a move, *so unconventional and daring that it rather took Halifax's breath away* – his intention to personally fly to Germany to negotiate with Hitler.[5] Chamberlain was convinced that if it came off, *it would go far beyond the present crisis and might prove the opportunity for bringing about a complete change in the international situation*.[6] At midnight on 13 September Chamberlain informed Hitler that he intended to fly to Germany personally to seek a peaceful solution to the Sudetenland question. He informed stunned Cabinet colleagues of 'Plan Z' the following morning, leading to an anxious wait until Hitler's reply later that afternoon inviting him and his wife to Berchtesgaden. Whether it was true or not Chamberlain believed that Hitler had been 'struck all of a heap' by his offer and exclaimed, 'I can't let a man of his age come all this way; I must go to London', which Chamberlain felt, *shows a side of Hitler that would surprise many people in this country*.[7] Chamberlain was not to be deprived of his diplomatic coup, though he was apprehensive not least because it was the first time he had ever been on an aeroplane. He was accompanied by his close advisor Sir Horace Wilson, the increasingly sceptical head of the central European section of the Foreign Office William Strang and the British Ambassador Sir Neville Henderson. The effect of Chamberlain's initiative was electrifying. Henry 'Chips' Channon was at a banquet when he heard the dramatic news. He recorded in his diary later that evening, 'It is one of the finest, most inspiring acts of all history. The company rose to their feet electrified, as all the world must be, and drank to his health. History must be ransacked to find a parallel. Of course a way out will now be found. Neville by his imagination and practical good sense, has saved the world. I am staggered.'[8]

Nazi Foreign Minister Joachim von Ribbentrop and Dr Herbert von Dirksen, German Ambassador in London, met Chamberlain at Munich airfield. Chamberlain was delighted with the *enthusiastic welcome of the crowds who were waiting in the rain & gave me the Nazi salute & shouted 'Heil' at the tops of their voices all the way along the station*. From Munich he made the three-hour train journey on Hitler's personal train to Berchtesgaden where Hitler was waiting for him on the steps of the Brown House. Recording his first impressions Chamberlain noted: *His hair is brown, not black, his eyes blue, his expression rather disagreeable, especially in repose and altogether he looks entirely undistinguished. You would never notice him in a crowd & would taken him for the house painter he once was*. After tea and some agonising small talk, Hitler, Chamberlain and their interpreters retired to an

Joachim von Ribbentrop (1893–1946), a former champagne salesman, joined the Nazi Party in 1932 and his aristocratic and foreign connections proved useful to Hitler. In 1933 he founded the Party's own foreign affairs bureau, negotiating the Anglo-German Naval Treaty independently of the Foreign Ministry, and was Ambassador to Britain from 1936 until 1938, when Hitler made him Foreign Minister. The outbreak of war sidelined diplomacy, and thus Ribbentrop. He was arrested by the Allies in 1945, found guilty at Nuremberg and hanged in 1946.

upstairs room *completely bare of ornament* to begin what turned out to be three hours of discussions. Chamberlain, *soon saw that the situation was much more critical than I had anticipated ... and it was clear that rapid decisions must be taken if the situation was to be saved*. Hitler lost no time in informing Chamberlain that the invasion of Czechoslovakia was imminent, in response to which Chamberlain *became indignant saying that I did not see why he had allowed me to come all this way and that I was wasting my time.* At this Hitler *quieted down* and said that if Chamberlain could assure him that the British government accepted the principle of self-determination he *was prepared to discuss ways & means.* This Chamberlain was unable to do without consulting the Cabinet though he informed Hitler of his personal opinion, *that on principle I didn't care two hoots whether the Sudetens were in the Reich or out of it, according to their own wishes but I saw immense difficulties in a plebiscite.* When discussions were over Hitler, *promised not to give the order to march unless some outrageous incident forced his hand.* Chamberlain believed the meeting to have been a significant success. Horace Wilson informed him that Hitler had been heard to remark afterwards that, *I have had a conversation with a* man, *he said, & one with whom I can do business & he liked the rapidity with which I grasped the essentials.* For his part Chamberlain believed, fatefully as it transpired, that, *I had established a certain confidence which was my aim and on my side in spite of the hardness & ruthlessness I thought I saw in his face I got the impression that here was a man who could be relied upon when he had given his word.*[9]

I got the impression that here was a man who could be relied upon when he had given his word.

CHAMBERLAIN ON HITLER

As far as Chamberlain was concerned 'Plan Z' was a resounding success. *I have still many anxious days before me, but the most gnawing anxiety is gone for I feel that I have nothing to reproach myself with & and that on the contrary up to now things are going the way I want.*[10] The country believed it too. Chamberlain was showered with letters of praise and gifts including gold watches and fishing rods. He saw Runciman and had over an hour with the King, *who sent me the most charming note*

& *was as excited as a boy*. He also had two Cabinets lasting five hours where he, *finally overcame all critics, some of whom had been concerting opposition beforehand*.[11] Despite the public mood the Cabinet was distinctly lacking in enthusiasm. Thomas Inskip noted in his diary later that evening that, 'the impression made by the PM's story was a little painful ... The PM said more than once to us that he was just in time. It was plain that Hitler had made the running: he had in fact blackmailed the PM.'[12] Indeed Berchtesgaden underlined the fact that Chamberlain had lost the initiative to Hitler. As subsequent events amply underlined, he never regained it.

Hitler meanwhile was delighted with the outcome. Whilst Chamberlain mistakenly believed that the meeting of Hitler's *strictly limited* territorial aims would be the end of Germany's claim on Czechoslovakian soil Hitler saw that his territorial ambitions could be realised through a short-term diplomatic solution to the 'Sudeten question' as a preface to the complete subjugation of Czechoslovakia. Whilst Chamberlain was parlaying with the King Hitler was ordering Henlein to form a Sudeten German Legion to wage terrorist attacks against the Czechs. That same day Daladier and Bonnet, the French Foreign Minister flew to London for discussions which lasted from 11 a.m. until after midnight. The proposals were then sent to the Czechs who only accepted this diplomatic *fait accompli* with extreme reluctance on 21 September. It was a fateful show of weakness by the western democracies for it revealed that, 'serious resistance was not to be expected from Britain; France would do what Britain did; the war was half-won. That was how Hitler saw it.'

Chamberlain flew to Germany for a second time on 22 September to meet an altogether less accommodating Hitler at the luxurious Hotel Dreesen in Bad Godesburg with its commanding views over the Rhine. Chamberlain was accommodated in the Petersburg Hotel on the opposite bank. Having reported how Hitler's demands at Berchtesgaden had been met, the Anglo-French guarantee of Czechoslovakia's borders and the possibility of a non-aggression pact with the Czechs Chamberlain was astonished to hear from Hitler that 'this solution no longer applies'. His new demand was the immediate occupation of the Sudetenland on 28 September. Chamberlain returned to his hotel depressed and angry. He refused to attend a meeting with Hitler scheduled for the following morning, sending him a letter stating that it was impossible for him to approve this new plan. Hitler merely reiterated his new demands, leaving Chamberlain with little choice but to offer these terms to the Czechs. A second meeting the following evening, lasting from 11 p.m. until 1.45 a.m., failed to persuade Hitler to moderate his stance. Hitler demanded the withdrawal of Czech troops within two days and completion in four. Chamberlain protested at this *ultimatum* stating that, *with great disappointment and deep regret I must register Herr Chancellor that you have not supported in the slightest my efforts to maintain peace*.[13] At this tense moment those assembled were informed that Beneš had ordered general mobilisation. Hitler promised to do nothing despite the 'provocation' and agreed to postpone his invasion until 1 October.

Chamberlain was somewhat less emollient upon his return and, having reported to Cabinet he dispatched Horace Wilson to Berlin on 26 September (together with Neville Henderson and Sir Ivone Kirkpatrick) explaining that, whilst he was sympathetic to the German position and was willing to expedite 'a quick solution' Hitler's terms and timeframe were 'wholly unacceptable' to both the Czechs and British public opinion.[14] Hitler was incandescent with rage. His translator later testified that he had never seen him so angry. Hitler reiterated his ultimatum, ranting at Wilson that 'if France and England want to strike, let them go ahead. I don't give a damn.'[15] That evening during his speech at the Berlin Sportsplast Hitler was, 'in the worst state of excitement I've ever seen him in,' recorded the journalist William Shirer. Wilson returned the next morning with a letter from Chamberlain guaranteeing that if Hitler refrain from using force the Czechs would be persuaded to withdraw from the Sudetenland. Hitler was beyond reasoning, informing Wilson that, 'it's a matter of complete indifference to me' whether England and France stood by the Czechs or not and that he was 'prepared for every eventuality'.[16] It was only because pressure was exerted upon Hitler, most notably by Göring and internationally by Mussolini, that the situation was pulled back from the brink on the morning of 28 September. The previous night Chamberlain had attempted to diffuse the situation with his famous speech that Britain would not go to war over *a quarrel in a faraway country between people of whom we know nothing*. He also wrote to Hitler expressing his astonishment that the *Führer* would be prepared to risk world war *for the sake of a few days* delay in settling this *long standing problem*. The letter also contained proposals, agreed in advance by the French, to persuade Czechs to hand over the Sudetenland, the transfer of which would be guaranteed by Britain and would begin on 1 October. Chamberlain also offered to come to Berlin to discuss proposals with Hitler.

A quarrel in a faraway country between people of whom we know nothing.

CHAMBERLAIN

Mussolini's mediation also allowed Hitler to avoid any humiliating climbdown. Exhausted, all Chamberlain could do now, however, was wait and hope that *all the prayers of all the peoples of the world including Germany herself*, would not, *break against the fanatical obstinacy of one man.*[17]

The last desperate snatch at the last tuft of grass on the very verge of the precipice, came on 28 September as Chamberlain was concluding his speech to the House of Commons on the current situation with regards to Czechoslovakia informing them that German mobilisation would commence at 2 p.m. that afternoon. The Royal Navy had been mobilised the day beforehand, gas masks were issued and anti-aircraft barrage balloons were set-up along the Embankment. War appeared imminent. At the height of his peroration Chamberlain was a handed a note by Sir John Simon announcing that Hitler would meet Chamberlain, Daladier and Mussolini the following day in Munich, details of which he immediately relayed to the House.[18] 'That, I think, was the one of the most dramatic moments which I have ever witnessed,' observed Harold Nicolson. 'For a second, the House was hushed in absolute silence. And then the whole House burst into a roar of cheering, since they knew that this might mean peace.' When Chamberlain sat down after his speech, 'the whole House rose as a man to pay tribute to his achievement.' Well almost. Nicolson himself impertinently remained seated until prompted by a fellow MP who hissed at him 'Stand up, you brute!'[19]

Chamberlain met Hitler, Mussolini and Daladier the following day at the newly-constructed Führerbau in Munich to begin dismembering Czechoslovakia. The Czechs were conspicuous by their absence. Mussolini, who had brokered the Munich agreement though the text was ostensibly Göring's, was 'bored' by the 'vaguely parliamentary air' of the proceedings.[20] Upon his arrival in Munich Chamberlain was immediately put at ease by friendly words from Hitler which, although he realised they could be deceptive, were, *so moderate and reasonable that I felt instant relief.*[21] He was soon to be disabused of any notion that concessions might be made to the Czechs, however. His attempts to gain compensation for the loss of Czech government property during the transfer was met with an angry retort from Hitler who told him: 'our time is for me too precious to waste it on such trivialities.'[22] With the rape of Czechoslovakia complete, those assembled retired for a festive dinner. Chamberlain and Daladier declined to join them. Presumably they had lost their appetite. Later that evening Chamberlain visited Hitler in his private apartment in Prinzregentenplatz to present him with a pre-prepared declaration for the two nations never to go to war again which Hitler signed only reluctantly, not that Chamberlain appears to have realised. Hitler was disappointed by Munich and felt cheated of his great triumph. Nevertheless, Munich allowed Hitler to gain the measure of his political opponents. He was not impressed. 'Our enemies are small worms' he told his generals prior to invading Poland in August 1939. 'I saw them in Munich.' No more would Hitler allow himself to become ensnared in diplomatic wrangling. Those who had counselled this course were left fatally weakened, leaving Hitler unfettered to pursue his drive to war.[23]

For Chamberlain Munich had entailed two days of *terrific physical and mental exertions ... one prolonged nightmare*, driving him to the very brink of a nervous breakdown.[24] During that moment, however, all his labours appeared worth it. Arriving home at Heston aerodrome Chamberlain reaffirmed to the assembled audience his belief that Munich represented the foundation of the peace process. *The settlement of the Czechoslovakian problem which has now been achieved is, in my view, only the prelude to a larger settlement in which all Europe may find peace*, Chamberlain remarked.[25] He then brandished the piece of paper containing his and Hitler's signatures and read out its contents. He was met with rapturous applause. *Even the descriptions of the papers gives no idea of the scenes in the streets as I drove from Heston to the Palace*, he wrote to his sister, *They were lined from one end to the other with people of every class, shouting themselves hoarse, leaping on the running board, banging on the windows & thrusting their hands into the car to be shaken.* Having met the King at Buckingham Palace Chamberlain returned home where, *I spoke to the multitudes below from the same window I believe as that from which Dizzy* [Benjamin Disraeli] *announced peace with honour* 60 years *ago* [following the Congress of Berlin in 1878].[26] It was during the course of this speech from the first-floor window of 10 Downing Street that Chamberlain uttered his immortal words: *My good friends, this is the second time in history that there has come from Germany to Downing Street peace with honour.* After the cheering had abated he continued, *I believe it is peace for our time.* The crowds greeted this with cries of 'We thank you. God bless you' before Chamberlain commanded them, *to go home and sleep quietly in your beds.*[27]

> *My good friends, this is the second time in history that there has come from Germany to Downing Street peace with honour. I believe it is peace for our time.*
>
> CHAMBERLAIN

Chamberlain had no doubt he had pacified Hitler and averted another World War. Others believed him too. The popular outpouring in favour of Chamberlain was immense, though Chamberlain resisted the temptation to call a snap general election, a course of action, which was being urged upon him by close colleagues like Ball. An *embarrassing profusion* of gifts arrived in the following weeks, crates of fine wine, fishing rods and tackle, watches, lucky horseshoes, tweed for sporting socks and suits. According to Lord Kemsley there were over 90,000 applications for the commemorative 'art plate' of the Chamberlains offered by the *Daily Sketch* for a coupon and 3d.[28] Within less than a month, however, popular clamour had faded and, *a lot of people seem to me to be losing their heads and talking and thinking as though Munich had made war more instead of less imminent.*[29] Nevertheless, despite Chamberlain's sanguine observation he continued to garner at least 70 letters of praise a day, a flow which continued *without much abatement* leading his wife *to engage extra help so that her and four paid secretaries can get through it all.*[30] Although Hitler almost immediately reneged on the terms of the Munich agreement, i.e. the promise of plebiscites and a guarantee to the rump of Czechoslovakia Chamberlain kept the House of Commons on side. Only Duff Cooper felt compelled to resign, though his departure failed to ruffle Chamberlain, whilst Oliver Stanley and Harry Crookshank, Secretary for Mines both retracted their resignations following Chamberlain's performance in the Commons debate on the Munich pact. Local Conservative Associations and Central Office stood squarely behind the Prime Minister against the 'anti-appeasers'.[31]

Those who continued to disagree with Chamberlain often found themselves smeared by *Truth*, a vehemently anti-Semitic and pro-Nazi newspaper secretly controlled by Chamberlain's close friend Sir Joseph Ball who also tapped the telephones of Chamberlain's critics, including Eden and Churchill, as part of his attempts since 1937 to mould a 'tame' British press incapable of antagonising Hitler and derailing Chamberlain's bid for *rapprochement*. Chamberlain was certainly alive to the advantages of media management. In the aftermath of Munich he dismantled the Foreign Office News Department, a source of anti-appeasement, making Downing Street the sole repository for Whitehall news, and through the aegis of George Steward, Downing Street's chief press liaison officer who, MI5 discovered, had told an official at the German Embassy that Britain would 'give Germany everything she asks for the next year'. He did so at the behest of Ball, quite possibly with Chamberlain's complicity despite his claim to be 'aghast' at the news when confronted by Halifax.[32] Chamberlain was also well versed in manipulating the lobby system in order to control the dissemination of news and thus journalists themselves, many of whom, enamoured of their privileged access to the Prime Minister, cravenly suspended their critical faculties in order to parrot the Chamberlainite line on news stories.[33]

Interpreting Chamberlain's motives at Munich are of pivotal importance in determining his legacy. Did he genuinely believe that Munich had pacified Europe or was he merely seeking to delay Hitler from being able to deal Britain, *a terrible, perhaps mortal blow*,[34] and in doing so purchasing time for further rearmament? If it were the latter then his Cabinet colleagues can be forgiven for not noticing and indeed lobbying for rearmament to be accelerated. Chamberlain believed his colleagues to be *losing their heads* and observed that:

> *A good deal of false emphasis has been placed on rearmament, as though one result of the Munich Agreement has been that it would be necessary for us to add to our rearmament programmes. Acceleration of existing programmes was one thing, but increases in the scope of our programme which would lead to a new arms race was a different proposition.*[35]

Believing he had won a lasting peace at Munich Chamberlain was loath to antagonise the dictators by assenting to such alarmist increases in defence expenditure. Lord Halifax also urged Chamberlain not only to step up the pace of rearmament but also to broaden the base of his government by offering to bring Labour into Cabinet and to facilitate the return of Eden. Chamberlain was reluctant to pursue either course because including Labour would make the discussion of international affairs *a constant running battle* whilst the return of Eden would be to invite further friction because, *at bottom he* [Eden] *is really dead against making terms with the dictators … he leaves out or chooses not to see for the moment that the conciliation part of the policy is just as important as rearming.* Although he was keen to enhance his support within the Cabinet rather than detract from it by appointing those *who would sooner or later wreck the policy with which I am identified*, Chamberlain equally refused to countenance calling a general election on the grounds that this was *bad tactics* though he acknowledged that he secretly longed to win a popular mandate for his policies.[36] Chamberlain effectively ignored Halifax's suggestions. He did, however, appoint Runciman as Lord President of the Council removing Lord Hailsham who had recently attacked Chamberlain's policy towards Czechoslovakia in the Cabinet on 25 September.

A further obstacle Chamberlain was keen to surmount was France which could undo all of his good work, drawing Britain into a war with Germany on their behalf if Anglo-French relations were mishandled. Determined to avoid this at all costs Chamberlain, Halifax and their wives travelled to France in an attempt to foster a climate of unity on 23 November to *strengthen Daladier* and also, rather arrogantly, *to give the French people an opportunity of pouring out their pent up feelings of gratitude and affection* towards himself.[37] But whilst Chamberlain made overtures to the French there were ominous rumblings from Germany. On 16 November 1938 Hitler made a snide references in his speech to Britain's 'umbrella carrying bourgeois' – widely agreed to be a contemptuous reference to Chamberlain – and two days later declared in Munich, 'there should be no surprise that we secure for ourselves our rights by another way if we cannot gain them by the normal way.' Chamberlain, however, heard what he wanted to hear, epitomised by reports from East Fulham MP Bill Astor that Hitler believed he could do 'business' with Chamberlain. Nevertheless Chamberlain was *horrified* by the Nazi 'Kristallnacht' pogrom and pondered that there seems to be, *some fatality about Anglo-German relations which invariably blocks every effort to improve them.*[38] Not that this dissuaded Chamberlain from continuing his strenuous efforts to appease Germany.

To compound matters Chamberlain was also suddenly confronted by an aggressive Italy, which, on 30 November, demanded the annexation of Nice, Corsica and Tunis from the French. Having observed the success of Hitler's 'Sudeten methods', Mussolini was determined to follow suit and bully the French into surrender. On 11 January 1939 Chamberlain, accompanied by Halifax for a personal *tête-à-tête* with Mussolini, which, although brief, filled Chamberlain with hope. It was a *truly wonderful visit* and Chamberlain waxed lyrical: *I consider I have achieved all I expected to get and more and that I am satisfied that the journey has definitely strengthened the chances of peace.* Chamberlain found Mussolini *straightforward and considerate* and with *a sense of humour which is quite attractive.* He was further beguiled by the *most astonishing enthusiasm* that everywhere greeted the British party on the streets of Italy, failing to realise the extent to which it was orchestrated.[39]

However, throughout the winter of 1938 the rumblings of discontent about the pace of rearmament and the direction of foreign policy both from his opponents and his supporters were beginning to take their toll on Chamberlain who, although not overly sympathetic to his critics was nevertheless beginning to feel the rub, particularly in Cabinet.[40] Shortly after his return from Italy Chamberlain made a speech in Birmingham on 28 January re-emphasising *defence not defiance* whilst appealing to Hitler that *the time has now come when others should make their contribution.* Horace Wilson supplied Hitler with an advance copy of the speech to assist him in formulating his own response two days later, which Neville Henderson in Berlin reported Hitler had subsequently altered to include reference to a 'long peace'. When it appeared that the dictators were prepared to play the diplomatic game Chamberlain's correspondence reveals that his ultimate objections were not to the aims of the dictators but their methods:

> *I think they had good cause to ask for consideration of their grievances, and if they had asked nicely after I appeared on the scene they might already have got some satisfaction … now it will take some time before the atmosphere is right, but things are moving in the direction I want.*[41]

Chamberlain was by now increasingly optimistic that *at last we are getting on top of the dictators* and believed that Hitler had *missed the bus* at Munich. This he believed had given Britain the time to detect its *weak points* and strengthen them as a result of which, *they could not make nearly such a mess of us now as they could have done then, while we could make much more of a mess of them. It is the same with the French.* Coupled with his own reading of the international situation Chamberlain felt that there was sufficient weight, *on the peace side of the balance* to enable him to take a firmer line with the dictators, *which some of my critics have applauded without apparently understanding the connection between diplomacy and strategic strength which nevertheless has been always stressed by the wisest diplomats and statesmen in the past.*[42] The Foreign Office too had failed to see the bigger picture as far as Chamberlain was concerned. *I simply cannot keep their minds fixed on our real purpose,* lamented Chamberlain, who believed that their dislike of totalitarianism was so strong, *that it will keep bursting out.* All of this left Chamberlain in no doubt *that we are getting near to a critical point where the whole future direction of European politics will be decided.* Mussolini in particular would have to be handled with *the utmost care and tact.*[43]

Chapter 6: The Failure of Appeasement

Hitler's occupation of Prague on 15 March 1939 threw the validity of appeasement into complete disarray. Having only just reported optimistically on the international situation to the press, Chamberlain appeared ridiculous. Following a muted speech in the House of Commons Chamberlain's authority momentarily ebbed away. 'All the tadpoles are beginning to swim in the other direction,' snorted Harold Nicolson.[1] He rallied two days later at Birmingham, however. *Is this the last attack upon a small State or is it to be followed by another? Is this in fact a step in the direction of an attempt to dominate the world by force*, asked Chamberlain rhetorically, and if so, he promised, Britain would, *take part to the utmost of its power in resisting such a challenge.*[2] At last Chamberlain appeared to recognise that Hitler was insatiable. Various voices suggested the crisis could be weathered if Chamberlain enlarged the Cabinet. Chamberlain resisted such suggestions, particularly the increasingly strident calls for Churchill's inclusion, though he recognised, *that the nearer we get to war the more his chances improve and vice versa.*[3] Chamberlain now turned his attention to constructing an alliance with Poland and the Soviet Union, opening up for Germany the possibility of a war on two fronts which would act as a deterrent and buy Chamberlain more time to rearm. This would thus put Britain in a stronger negotiating position, a strong indication that Chamberlain was continuing to chase the chimera of appeasement.

The decision to try and build an alliance with Russia and a wider four-power declaration was a leap of faith for Chamberlain who harboured a *profound distrust* of the Soviet Union.[4] As his Private Secretary Douglas-Home recalled in 1962: 'Chamberlain ... saw Communism as the major long-term danger. He hated Hitler and German Fascism, but he felt that Europe in general and Britain in particular were in even greater danger from Communism.'[5] Chamberlain also believed that Russia desired to stand aside whilst everyone else fought it out. *Our problem therefore is to keep Russia in the background without antagonising her*, Chamberlain observed.[6] Chamberlain regarded Russia as an unreliable military partner, poorly equipped and fatally weakened by Stalin's purges, who *would fail us in an extremity*, and only wished he had been able *to have taken a much stronger line with them all through, but I could not have carried my colleagues with me*.[7] Chamberlain's diplomacy, initially given a greater sense of urgency by a false rumour that the Nazis were preparing to invade Romania, soon ran aground, however, on the very real Polish fear, expressed by Colonel Jozef Beck, that an overt alliance with Soviet Russia made them more, not less, likely to be the victim of German aggression. Smaller states like Romania and Finland were equally hostile. The Poles were similarly resistant to Chamberlain's overtures concerning Nazi demands for the port of Danzig. As hope for a four-power declaration collapsed, Chamberlain received a further jolt when the Germans occupied the Baltic port of Memel on 21 March and Mussolini invaded Albania on 7 April. The only alternative to allowing Germany to carve up the smaller states was to issue Hitler an ultimatum, which Chamberlain refused to countenance:

We are not strong enough ourselves & we cannot command sufficient strength elsewhere to present Germany with overwhelming force. Our ultimatum would therefore mean war and I would never be responsible for presenting it. We should have to go on rearming & collecting what help we could from outside in the hope that something would happen to break the spell, either Hitler's death or a realisation that the defence was too strong to make attack feasible.[8]

The Cabinet was still contemplating whether or not to guarantee Poland when Ian Colvin, Berlin correspondent of the *News Chronicle*, delivered news of the impending invasion of Poland, receiving further validation on 29 March from the British military attaché in Berlin. An emergency Cabinet meeting was hastily convened on 30 March and the following day Chamberlain guaranteed Polish sovereignty, 'in the event of any action which clearly threatened Polish independence'. This was a *big decision*, noted Chamberlain.[9] Only *The Times* noticed that Chamberlain's statement was, 'concerned with not the boundaries of states but attacks on their independence. And it is we who will judge whether their independence is threatened or not.' Polish territorial integrity was most certainly not safeguarded. Hitler responded on 1 April with a speech warning pointedly against 'encirclement'.[10] Chamberlain recognised that Hitler *finds it so easy to tear up treaties and throw overboard assurances that no one can feel any confidence in new ones from him and he has so managed his affairs as to create an atmosphere in which further discussion with him would command no support in this country.* He remained confident, however, of finding *the best way of keeping Master Hitler quiet* and continued his penchant for amateur interventions rather than the professional diplomacy of the Foreign Office.[11] Negotiations with Russia concerning an alliance led by Sir

William Strang of the Foreign Office dragged on interminably throughout the summer of 1939 until 4 August when it was suddenly announced that Russia had signed the Nazi-Soviet pact. Chamberlain's belief *about it not altering things* was short-lived.[12] In the face of all the available evidence Chamberlain, who felt *like a man driving a clumsy coach over a narrow crooked road along the face of a precipice*, remained convinced peace was possible, despite the breakdown of talks between Germany and Poland about Danzig. He was also dismissive of security service reports predicting an imminent invasion of Poland because, *they haven't marched yet and, as always, I count every hour that passes without a catastrophe as adding its might to the slowly accumulating anti-war forces.*[13] His optimism proved misplaced.

When Germany invaded Poland on 1 September Chamberlain delayed the declaration of war for 48 hours, to allow the French more time to mobilise and for their Foreign Minister Bonnet to covertly try and reach a deal with Mussolini for a second 'Munich'. The delay did little credit to Chamberlain's reputation or indeed those of the members of his Cabinet. On 3 September Chamberlain reluctantly declared *this country is at war with Germany*. His announcement was followed by the soothing sounds of cellist Beatrice Harrison performing 'Caprice and Elegy'. As Lord Blake observed, however, 'even then his summoning the nation to arms sounded a cracked and wavering note. He seemed more concerned at the collapse of his personal policy and all that he had stood for than at the critical situation that he led.'[14] The outbreak of the Second World War was, like Andros over 40 years earlier, a crushing personal failure for Chamberlain. The BBC radio announcer present when Chamberlain declared war, Alvar Lidell, never forgot the experience of, 'sitting there, behind this figure of terrible grief'.[15] At that moment Chamberlain's cup of misery overflowed. *Everything that I have worked for, everything that I have hoped for, everything that I have believed in during my public life, has crashed into ruins*,

he lamented to the House of Commons. Though it was not immediately apparent at the time, amongst the ruins was his historical reputation. *There is only one thing left for me to do*, Chamberlain stated, *that is, to devote what strength and powers I have to forwarding the victory of the cause for which we have sacrificed so much.*[16]

Everything that I have worked for,
everything that I have hoped for,
everything that I have believed in during
my public life, has crashed into ruins.

CHAMBERLAIN

Dazed and confused, Chamberlain was still not quiet able to believe that Hitler had been *talking through his hat*. As he wrote to his sister a week later, *It is only a fortnight since I wrote to you last but it seems to me like seven years. In such days of stress and strain one loses all sense of time. One day is life another & Sundays are only more trying than other days – and like is just one long nightmare.* Chamberlain was also acutely conscious that his time as Prime Minister was nearing an end. Having always previously felt *indispensable* Chamberlain now recognised that, *half a dozen people could take my place while war is in progress and I do not see that I have any particular part to play until it comes to discussing peace terms – and that may be a long way off …*[17] Chamberlain was no war leader. He lacked strategic vision for one thing. Chamberlain did not believe that Hitler would attack the Maginot Line or violate Dutch and Belgian neutrality – *I reject that alternative* – and although he felt an air offensive likely he was convinced that developments in British radar facilities and fighter plane technology rendered German success *extremely doubtful*. Indeed he was still not persuaded of the need for an offensive war. *What we ought to do is just to throw back the peace offer and continue the blockade. In a waiting war of that kind I believe we could outlast the Germans*, he wrote. The war would be over by spring, Chamberlain reassured himself.[18]

The New Year, however, ushered in not the end of the war but the climax of a bitter dispute between War Minister Leslie Hore-Belisha and Lord Gort of the British Expeditionary Force, which Chamberlain was called upon to resolve. In the event Hore-Belisha rather petulantly left the government rather than accept Chamberlain's offer of a post at the Board of Trade. Chamberlain's mood darkened further with news of the Soviet invasion of Finland but refused to *do their dirty work* by conveying the Russian peace terms.[19] Although Chamberlain remained convinced Hitler could be defeated by economic pressure, his belief that widespread bloodshed was avoidable went right down to the wire, until that is the *Wehrmacht* overran Denmark and Norway.

Chamberlain's political and physical demise were almost simultaneous. 'He fell in May, in July he was stricken by illness, he died in November,' noted his official biographer succinctly.[20] On 3 May 1940 the right-wing journalist Collin Brooks noted in his diary 'What fools we British are at the beginning of any war, is the kind of

The Norwegian campaign of April–June 1940 arose out of the Allies' desire to tighten the economic blockade on Germany by halting the supply of Swedish iron ore to Germany via the Norwegian port of Narvik. In the event, Hitler forestalled the planned British landings by mounting an invasion of his own on 9 April 1940. Both sides suffered heavy naval losses, but the last Allied troops were withdrawn from Narvik on 8 June. However, the threat of another Allied invasion of Norway kept large numbers of German troops tied up there for the rest of the war, some 250,000 surrendering there in 1945 without firing a shot.

reflection on most people's lips, with a snarl at Chamberlain. Poor Chamberlain has had more of "Hosanna-today; crucify him tomorrow" than anybody since Christ I should imagine – not that he is a particularly Christ-like person.'[21] Although it was Churchill who masterminded the disastrous Norwegian expedition to Narvik, it was Chamberlain who was held responsible, much to the former's astonishment. Only days before he had told the Conservative Central Council that Hitler had *missed the bus*, an unfortunate expression hardly likely to instil confidence in his judgement.[22] Indeed as the government's stock plummeted a two-day debate took place in the House of Commons on 7 and 8 May. It was *a very painful affair* for Chamberlain whose leadership was assailed from all sides.[23] It was made all the more painful by the Conservative MP Leo Amery who, echoing the immortal words of

'The fact is that our party … won't have you and I think I am right in saying the country won't have you either.'

ATTLEE TO CHAMBERLAIN

Oliver Cromwell to the Long Parliament urged him, 'You have sat too long here for any good you have been doing. Depart, I say, and let us have done with you. In the name of God, go.'[24] Chamberlain won the debate by 281 to 200 votes, a comfortable majority of 81 votes, but 33 government supporters had backed the Opposition and there had been more than 60 abstentions.

For the moment, however, Chamberlain still maintained his grip on power. Those who voted against him, like the young John Profumo MP, were hauled before an incandescent Chief Whip David Margesson who concluded a vitriolic tirade against him thus: 'And I can tell you this, you utterly contemptible little shit. On every morning that you wake up for the rest of your life, you will be ashamed of what you did last night.'[25] Over the course of the next few days it became

The Premiership

There are two important changes to the role of the Prime Minister, which are connected to Chamberlain's time in office. Peter Hennessy notes in his book *Prime Minister* that Tony Blair fended off the request of Dr Tony Wright, the Chairman of the Public Administration Committee of the House of Commons, to appear in front of them with a curt reply: 'As you know, evidence to Select Committees is normally provided by "line" departments or via a Government memorandum. Prime Ministers have not themselves, by long-standing convention, given evidence to Select Committees. That remains the position." The Cabinet Office primed No. 10 on how to fend off Wright's assertion of all-party select committee power. They rested on the argument that when premiers ceased to be Leader of the House of Commons during the Second World War select committees lost the power to summon them. The last premier to appear, Neville Chamberlain, had gone as Leader of the House not Prime Minister. This was the defence 70, Whitehall provided for the Prime Minister's Office. [Peter Hennessy, *The Prime Minister* (Penguin, London: 2000) p 531.]

'When Churchill replaced Neville Chamberlain as Prime Minister in May 1940, his predecessor kept a seat in the War Cabinet as Lord President of the Council and chaired the Cabinet in Churchill's absence. By the autumn of that year his worsening cancer was increasingly keeping Chamberlain away from the Cabinet Room. On 2 October 1940 the Secretary of the War Cabinet, Sir Edward Bridges, minuted Churchill about the "order of precedence" in the War Cabinet which placed Chamberlain ahead of Attlee who was Lord Privy Seal. "By tradition and long practice", Bridges told the Prime Minister, "there is an order of precedence among offices of Cabinet rank. But it is clearly established that the Prime Minister can settle the order of Cabinet Ministers *for Cabinet purposes* as he pleases ... The main question is who you want to preside over the War Cabinet when you are away." ... Bridges' reply marks the moment when, *de facto* (to borrow his words), the deputy premiership was created in reality.' [Peter Hennessy, *The Hidden Wiring* (Gollancz, London: 1995) pp 19f.]

increasingly clear to Chamberlain that Labour would no longer serve under him. Indeed Attlee told him bluntly that 'the fact is that our party ... won't have you and I think I am right in saying the country won't have you either.'[26] Recognising that, *the time had come for a National Government in the broadest sense* and *I knew that I could not get it* Chamberlain sought to gain official confirmation of the Labour attitude, *if only to justify my resignation to my own party*.[27] Having received official confirmation it was only left to find a successor. Chamberlain and the King both favoured Lord Halifax, who was not inclined to accept the offer, preferring a trip to the dentist instead of meeting with Chamberlain's emissary.[28] Later that day Chamberlain learned that Labour wanted Churchill, leaving him with little choice but to propose Churchill's name to the King whilst tendering his resignation which he publicly announced at 9 a.m. on 10 May 1940, by which time the Nazi war machine was tearing through Belgium and Holland towards France. Later that day Chamberlain talked with the defeatist American Ambassador Joseph Kennedy who told him that he did not believe that Britain could carry on without the French. *I told him I did not see how we could either*, Chamberlain noted in his diary.[29]

Although *my world has tumbled to bits in a moment*, Chamberlain was relieved to be spared the *agony of mind* that accompanied being a war leader a role for which, his entirely understandable momentary collapse into defeatism underlined, he was profoundly unsuited.[30] He was unable to detach himself entirely, however. Churchill, seeking to unite the party behind him, offered Chamberlain the post of Lord President of the Council with a seat in Cabinet allowing him to retain, significantly, the leadership of the party though opposition from Labour prevented him from assuming Leadership of the House of Commons. Although he was glad to no longer be burdened with the responsibility of leadership anymore, Chamberlain continued to harbour hopes of returning to Number 10 after what he presumed would be a short war.[31] Chamberlain and Churchill developed a successful and harmonious partnership, which allowed Chamberlain to exercise a large degree of executive control over domestic affairs for which Churchill was eternally grateful. 'To a very large extent I am in your hands,' he conceded to Chamberlain, 'and I feel no fear of that.' Indeed only a week after his own resignation Chamberlain was asked to 'mind the shop' and deputise for Churchill in Cabinet. As attacks against him reached a crescendo Chamberlain offered to resign. Churchill would have none of it, commanding Chamberlain's critics to desist for the sake of unity. 'Magically' the attacks ceased the following day.[32] Chamberlain was also a staunch ally of his Labour critics and even Attlee warmed to him, judging him to be, 'very able and crafty, and free from any of the rancour he might well have felt against us. He worked very hard and well: a good chairman, a good committeeman, always very businesslike. You could work with him.'[33]

But Chamberlain was not a well man. In the middle of June, in the aftermath of the fall of France and the British evacuation at Dunkirk – not yet transformed from perilous debacle into national victory – Chamberlain recorded that he was in *considerable pain* and in July X-rays revealed that he had a cancerous stricture of the bowel. Chamberlain knew his days were numbered both physically and politically. He continued in government but he knew that after Dunkirk his Labour colleagues *have considerably revised their ideas of my value in the government.*[34] On 22 September he tendered his resignation, which was reluctantly accepted by Churchill on 30 September. As a mark of respect Churchill offered to grant him the Order of the Garter but Chamberlain stated his wish replied that he would, *prefer to die plain 'Mr Chamberlain' like my father before me, unadorned by any title.*[35] Chamberlain died in his sleep on 9 November at his country home, Heckfield House, near the village of Odiham, Hampshire. Upon hearing of his death 'Chips' Channon recorded in his diary: 'Mr Chamberlain died in the night; in a way, though I loved him, I am glad: the shafts of malice had hurt him, and probably killed him ... He had nothing more to live for; all his hopes had gone.'[36] As soon as his news of his death became known in Birmingham 'the whole city appeared to go into mourning'.[37] Chamberlain was buried at Westminster Abbey on 14 November 1940. Churchill and the Cabinet acted as his pallbearers, reflecting the esteem in which he was still held by many political colleagues.

Part Three

THE LEGACY

Chapter 7: Chamberlain and the Battle for History

History has not been kind to Neville Chamberlain. His reputation was sealed by Munich, an event summed up for many by Norman Davies's pithy observation: 'under pressure from the ruthless the clueless combined with the spineless to achieve the worthless.'[1] Whether it is 'fair' to judge Chamberlain's entire political career solely by the last three years of his life from 1937 to 1940 or, even more narrowly, from September 1938 to May 1940, thereby ignoring or downplaying his role as a committed and progressive social reformer is in many ways completely irrelevant. To evaluate Chamberlain's historical reputation by any other criterion appears faintly ludicrous. These were the years, in Lord Blake's compelling judgment, when Chamberlain 'risked the whole existence of the nation'.[2] The stakes were high and the narrow margin by which the Battle of Britain was won indicates that it was a gamble he almost lost. Chamberlain had never meant to postpone war, he meant to avoid it indefinitely. In this quest he failed so very conspicuously.

His achievements prior to 1937 should certainly be born in mind, however. As his entry in the *Oxford Dictionary of National Biography* observes: 'Had Chamberlain retired in 1937 he would not have risked anything. He would have been a considerable figure in British political history, his career a study in success.'[3] But Chamberlain did not retire. He accepted the premiership imagining it to be his crowning glory. As it transpired it was his most bitter personal and political defeat. Thus was the 'authentic Chamberlain'[4] – the sincere social reformer – almost entirely obliterated from the popular consciousness by both subsequent history and historiography. There is little doubt Chamberlain himself would have preferred to be remembered for his domestic merits rather than his spectacular international failure. But given his personal identification with appeasement and his messianic belief that he alone could secure peace, how then, in all good conscience, can the historian evaluate Chamberlain using any other yardstick? It was Chamberlain himself who set the bar of history so very high. Indeed Chamberlain never let his opponents forget that appeasement was his personal policy. When reacting to criticisms levied at him in the disastrous aftermath of Norway in May 1940 it was Chamberlain who personalised the issue by calling on his *friends* to support him, which smacked of cynical partisanship and turned the debate into a personal vote of confidence, which he lost.[5] Chamberlain's legacy remains a hostage to historical fortune, intimately bound to Hitler and the Second World War to the extent that it is unlikely that he will ever enjoy a complete rehabilitation. But before the first stone is cast it is well to examine how others have cast theirs.

On 12 November 1940 the House of Commons gathered 'under the shadow of bereavement' to hear Churchill's eulogy to the recently deceased Neville Chamberlain. Chamberlain remained highly esteemed by many of his parliamentary colleagues and this continuing respect was reflected in Churchill's peroration, suffused as it was with a keen awareness of the extent to which his predecessor's past achievements had already been overshadowed by recent events. Churchill took a magnanimous long view of Chamberlain's career, reminding his listeners that, 'in one phase men might seem to have been right: in another they seemed to have been wrong, and then, when the perspective of time had lengthened, all stood in a different setting. There was a new proportion; there was another set of scales.'[6] Churchill's analysis was astute and, as David Dutton has so lucidly demonstrated, Chamberlain's reputation, posthumous or otherwise, has passed through several distinct historical cycles.[7]

Following his fall from grace in May 1940 Chamberlain's descent into obloquy was almost as meteoric as his rise. Rather than reflect upon his own errors and misjudgements – such as the delay in declaring war, holding Churchill at arm's length despite his rising popularity, his failure to sufficiently enlarge his Cabinet and to put the government onto a full war footing – all of which had eroded his own authority, Chamberlain preferred instead to view his present unpopularity as part of an orchestrated campaign by the Left rather than a reflection of the genuine antipathy his craven appeasement of Hitler had generated after the occupation of Prague. *People who have been building up a 'hate' against me have not in any way given up,* opined Chamberlain to his sister Ida.[8] The climax of this 'hate' campaign against Chamberlain arrived on 5 July 1940 with the publication of *Guilty Men*, a searing indictment of Chamberlain and his ossified predecessors. Three journalists working for the Beaverbrook press – Peter Howard, Frank Owen and Michael Foot – wrote *Guilty Men* under the collective pseudonym 'Cato'. Lord Beaverbrook, whose name was conveniently omitted from the list of the guilty, undoubtedly had a hand in it. Foot even reviewed *Guilty Men* in the *Evening Standard* to throw enquiring minds off the scent of its authorship. *Guilty Men* was a savage polemic, written fast and furiously shortly after the defeat of

France and the evacuation of the British Expeditionary Force from Dunkirk, which contemporaneously represented not a historic victory but a dangerous and humiliating military defeat leaving Britain isolated and alone in the fight against Nazi Germany. Thus *Guilty Men*, which excoriated Chamberlain for leading a woefully unprepared not to mention ill-equipped Britain to the 'edge of national humiliation', caught the national mood. Despite being banned from W H Smiths and Wyman's it sold over 200,000 copies. In private Waldorf Astor was clear that Chamberlain, 'a very capable mediocrity ... incapable of greatness or Statesmanship ... with no vision,' was to blame because, resting on his laurels after Munich, which he regarded as a triumph in itself, he had been 'unable to grasp the need for full urgent rearmament'. It is hard to exaggerate the importance of *Guilty Men*, which functioned as a literary people's court publicly delivering a verdict on the government's lamentable performance that the lack of a general election since 1935 had prevented the public from doing.[9]

Whether it was fair assessment or not, one thing is indisputable: *Guilty Men* gravely wounded Chamberlain's reputation. It would be no exaggeration to say that it is a blow from which it has yet to recover. Despite public statements to the contrary Chamberlain was indeed increasingly worried about the level to which his reputation had sunk, writing to his sister on 20 July 1940:

By the way does it occur to you when you read of the 'Men of Munich who brought us into this mess' that the exploits of the Navy R.A.F. & B.E.F. must have been made possible by the 'Men of Munich'? For no one can suppose that our equipment has all been turned out in the last six weeks. However, it would be foolish to expect from these blind partisans either reason or logic since those things are not allowed to interfere with their emotions.[10]

Chamberlain remained suitably piqued the following week when, in the privacy of a meeting of the National Union Executive he laid bare his irritation for all to see:

'He said that as far as he personally was concerned, he did not care a brass farthing, but as Leader of the Conservative Party his reputation did matter. It does not to do have the Leader of the Party discredited, and therefore, he wanted to say one or two words. The fact that the suggestion or out not having more tanks, aircraft and guns, and other equipment, was the responsibility of the present Leader of the Conservative Party, was not true. Everybody must share the responsibility for this state of affairs.'[11]

Baldwin presumed that Chamberlain's nerves might have finally given way during 1940. Not so, retorted Chamberlain. *Never for one single instant,* he replied, *have I doubted the rightness of what I did at Munich nor can I believe that it was possible for me to do more than I did to prepare the country for war after Munich, given the violent and persistent opposition I had to fight against.*[12]

Indeed Chamberlain remained adamant that, *if we had called Hitler's bluff* [in 1938] *and he had called ours, I do not think we could have survived a week.* Chamberlain remained unrepentant for Munich in the same way that he *never regretted*

Never for one single instant have I doubted the rightness of what I did at Munich nor can I believe that it was possible for me to do more than I did to prepare the country for war after Munich.

CHAMBERLAIN

the British guarantee to Poland. Quite simply Chamberlain believed he had done everything possible both to avert war and by the same token that he had done everything to prepare for it.[13]

But as Chamberlain continued to robustly defend himself against his critics so too were the seeds being sown of a historical defence that would later blossom into a whole canon of revisionist literature. Despite his obvious exasperation Chamberlain pretended serenity, content in the knowledge that, *although I have in a sense failed in everything I set out to achieve, I do not believe that history will blame me for that and I don't regard my public life as a failure.*[14] Chamberlain's loyal confident and Conservative Party dirty tricks expert Sir Joseph Ball was less sure, however. Well aware that history is rather easier to make than to unmake, Ball urged Chamberlain to allow him to begin a campaign to countermand the proponents of the *Guilty Men* thesis. As Ball noted: 'The first step in the operations must be a complete and devastating exposure of what is happening, accompanied by an equally pungent and forceful exposure of the vendetta and of the true facts of the situation as it has developed during the last six or seven years, and particularly during the last three years. If you agree that I am right, I will work out a plan of operations for your approval: and I should be prepared if necessary to resign from my present post for the purpose of carrying it out.'[15]

Close to death, Chamberlain displayed the same certitude that had characterised his life. Declining Ball's generous offer, in a long letter to his friend Chamberlain wrote that:

So far as my personal reputation is concerned, I am not in the least bit disturbed about it. The letters which I am still receiving in such vast quantities so unanimously dwell on the same point, namely without Munich the war would have been lost and the Empire destroyed in 1938 ... I do not feel the opposite view ... has a chance of survival. Even if nothing further were to be published giving the true inside story of the past two years, I should not fear the historian's verdict.[16]

It was a position he maintained until his death a few weeks later. Ironically Chamberlain's attitude mirrored that of another Prime Minister who at the turn of the century, convinced of his own rightness in taking the country into a deeply unpopular war, dismissed wide-ranging criticism of his conduct by referring to a higher celestial power as his judge. Who after all can argue with that?

Chamberlain's reputation was itself in need of some divine intervention following the mauling it took at the hands of *Guilty Men*. In its editorial two days after his death *The Times* asserted that, 'it is a pretty safe prediction that with the fuller disclosure of the truth which time will bring the stature of Neville Chamberlain will increase rather than diminish.'[17] It was not until after the end of the Second World War, however, that an effective defence of his reputation began to be mounted, spearheaded by his fiercely loyal surviving family. In between there were a several attempts at defending Chamberlain's political legacy most notably, Derek Walker-Smith's rather hurried *Neville Chamberlain* (1940). W W Hadley's *Munich: Before and After* (1944) and Viscount Maugham's *The Truth about the Munich Crisis* (1944) both defended appeasement and the Munich agreement and both predictably flew below the cultural and political radar. Quintin Hogg's *The Left Never Was Right* (1945), a vehement defence of the Conservative record, similarly failed to mitigate the impact of *Guilty Men* on popular consciousness.[18]

As early as 1941, however, the Chamberlain family were considering their posthumous response to what they regarded as the calumny of *Guilty Men*. Having considered distinguished historians like E H Carr, G M Young and Arthur Bryant for the task, Chamberlain's widow finally chose the Oxford don Keith Feiling who had assisted Churchill with his life of Marlborough and the first volume of his *History of the English-Speaking Peoples*, not to mention tutoring his son, Randolph. Feiling, who was given full access to Chamberlain's diaries and letters, completed his task in 1944 though it was not published until 1946. Although sympathetic to Chamberlain, Feiling had reservations about whether to accept the project, a hesitancy compounded by the absence of documentary evidence outside Chamberlain's personal papers. Once Chamberlain's redoubtable sisters had overcome their own doubts about Feiling and what Dutton refers to as 'his rather idiosyncratic prose style', Feiling was commissioned. *The Life of Neville Chamberlain* which drew on Chamberlain's personal papers and interviews with close colleagues including Churchill – no mean achievement the midst of total war – represented a monumental achievement given the political climate, a brave and controversial defence of a deeply unpopular contemporary political figure. The Chamberlain family themselves were broadly satisfied even if contemporary reviewers and former colleagues were not always enthralled by the picture Feiling had painted. The biography took four 'legends' to task: Chamberlain's hostility to the concept of collective security, his inherent sympathy for Nazi Germany, his steely-eyed determination not to deal with the Soviet Union and his failure to start, if not outright opposition to, rearmament.[19] Although there is a kernel of truth in each of these charges none of them are sustainable when put in so simplistic a manner. It is a testament to Feiling's scholarship that although his biography is overtly sympathetic to Chamberlain he succeeded in avoiding producing a hagiography. Indeed it remains a standard text over half a century later, its influence clearly visible on Chamberlain's recent entry in the *Oxford Dictionary of National Biography*. Its stature as a biography partly responsible the hostile comment surrounding the publication of Ian MacLeod's biography in

1961 which, as A J P Taylor stated contemptuously 'adds nothing' to the existing canon of historical knowledge. Given that Feiling had certainly massaged his subject to make him appear more amenable than he was, leaving out some of his more harsh criticisms of figures like Baldwin, MacLeod, as his own biographer conceded, had certainly missed an opportunity to deliver a more searching biographical portrait.[20]

Feiling's attempted rehabilitation of Chamberlain was hampered from the outset, however, by his denial of access to official papers, which he could have seen had he but realised. That he did not see them was due to Sir Edward Bridges, the Cabinet Secretary, with encouragement from Churchill who, considering writing his own memoirs, did not desire the competition. Churchill bade Bridges to obstruct Feiling's access which he did using a combination of pedantry and masterly inactivity which resulted in the impoverishment Feiling's biography, preventing a more rounded assessment of its subject as a political figure. *The Life of Neville Chamberlain* was finally published in December 1946 by which time the revisionist camp had only just begun to set out its stall when it received a devastating blow in the form of the first volume of Churchill's own florid war memoirs. *The Gathering Storm*, published in 1948, enabling Churchill to mould public perceptions of the appeasement, past and future, which in conjunction with *Guilty Men* sounded the literary death-knell for Chamberlain's reputation. That it also bolstered Churchill's image as a visionary seer for posterity was not coincidental either.[21]

This was not, however, Churchill's view at the time. Three days after Chamberlain's death Churchill paid tribute to him in a fulsome eulogy delivered in the House of Commons on 12 November 1940 in which he stated:

'Whatever else history may or may not say about these terrible, tremendous years, we can be sure that Neville

Chamberlain acted with perfect sincerity according to his lights and strove to the utmost capacity and authority, which were powerful, to save the world from the awful, devastating struggle in which we are now engaged. This alone will stand him in good stead as far as what is called the verdict of history is concerned.'[22]

Many of the myths propagated in *The Gathering Storm* continue to be recycled to this day not least in the recent BBC production of the same title. Further grist to the mill was added in 1964 with the publication of *The Appeasers* by Martin Gilbert and Richard Gott which offered a similarly withering indictment of appeasement, though Gilbert at least offered a partial revision of this thesis in *The Roots of Appeasement* published two years later which, as its title suggests, recast appeasement within its longer historical framework.

It was during the 1960s that the historiography of British political history began to shift from examining the failures of British foreign policy in terms of Chamberlain's personal responsibility vis-à-vis *Guilty Men* and *The Gathering Storm* to an awareness of the structural constraints that inhibited Chamberlain and his colleagues' room for manoeuvre. It would be fair to say that this approach generated an altogether more complex and favorable portrait of Chamberlain than had previously existed, one which cast appeasement in terms of diplomatic tradition rather than as the misguided brainchild of Chamberlain alone. Indeed Self argues Chamberlain practiced a 'shrewd realpolitik' in response to the complex strategic dilemmas facing an isolated island any one of which threatened to overwhelm Britain's already over-stretched imperial interests and hasten the demise of the British Empire and thus Britain as a world power.[23]

By the mid-1980s this more nuanced and sophisticated approach to Chamberlain's career had acquired more historiographical purchase over many of the Churchillian myths that had dominated since 1945. This revisionist approach reached its apogee at the end of the decade with the publication of *Chamberlain and the Lost Peace* (1989) by John Charmley, who believed Chamberlain's was, 'the only policy which offered hope of avoiding war'. Furthermore, stated Charmley, 'not even the edifice erected by Churchill could survive unscathed that opening of the records which, Chamberlain hoped, would explain his policy. The "Guilty Men" syndrome has run its course, and Chamberlain's reputation stands better now than it had even done.' Consumed by historical hubris Charmley confidently predicted that Chamberlain's historical standing would only improve.[24] Charmley rammed home this thesis in *Churchill: The End of Glory* (1993), which developed Chamberlain's own conviction that American involvement in the war would cause Britain to pay *too dearly* in the post-war settlement, which was deliberately designed to curtail British imperial and global power.[25] That appeasement sought to avoid a war that ultimately saw the decline of British power was for a new generation of historians a powerful argument for its re-evaluation. Charmley went so far as to argue that going to war in 1939 was wrong, as was Churchill's failure to make peace with Hitler in 1940 and again in 1941. Thus Churchill not Chamberlain becomes the 'Guilty Man'. Appeasement 'offered the only way of preserving what was left of British power,' wrote Charmley. 'If 1945 represented "victory", it was, as Chamberlain had foreseen, for the Soviets and the Americans.'[26] Such an argument drew a stinging rebuke from John Lukacs who assailed Charmley's flawed and preposterous thesis as 'denigration by a pampleteer' dependent as it was, according to Lukacs, upon limited knowledge, selective arguments and spurious evidence drawn from, amongst other sources, the disgraced historian and Holocaust denier David Irving.[27]

Charmley's overblown attempt to vindicate Chamberlain marked the high tide of the revisionist historical drive. Whether by design or default many revisionist histories published during the 1980s portrayed successive inter-war British governments as impotent actors imprisoned within the vortex of historical events. This may have dispelled many of the assumptions about Chamberlain emanating from the pens of 'Cato' and Churchill but it also diminished Chamberlain and his colleagues as historical figures, in effect infantilising them, denying that there were choices to be made and somebody, in this case Chamberlain, took personal responsibility for making them. One of the most startling contributions to the post-revisionist school came from Canadian scholar Sidney Aster who, like Feiling, used Chamberlain's personal papers and diaries to draw radically different conclusions; namely that Chamberlain's correspondence exhibited, 'misplaced trust, unwarranted optimism and erroneous judgments', all of which pointed to the conclusion that, 'the accusations spelled out by "Cato" in 1940 were in fact largely justified'.[28] The most erudite exponent of the thesis that alternatives were in fact open to Chamberlain was made by noted Oxford scholar R A C Parker in his extremely persuasive and nuanced study *Chamberlain and Appeasement* (1993), which argued that appeasement was not in fact the only course open to Chamberlain. Continued conciliation of Hitler was a conscious choice when in fact, after March 1938, Britain could have united with France to contain Germany through the aegis of the League of Nations covenant. In essence Parker felt that Chamberlain's 'powerful, obstinate personality', not

'Chamberlain's and Churchill's objectives were identical. Both intended to preserve the independence of Britain and its Empire. Their methods were totally different.'

R A C PARKER

to mention his skill in debate, rejected 'effective deterrence' in favour of appeasement, thus ultimately making war more likely, not less.[29] Parker's work was not an attempt to turn back the historiographical clock, however. *The Times* reviewer noted that it was 'a scrupulously scholarly synthesis designed to demolish both the original myth and the revisionist fantasy … compelling'.[30]

In a subsequent volume entitled *Churchill and Appeasement* (2000), Parker took as his starting point the preface to *The Gathering Storm* in which he related a conversation Churchill had had with President Roosevelt during the course of which, 'he told me that he was publicly asking for suggestion about what the war should be called. I said at once "The Unnecessary War". There never was a more easy war to stop.' Parker notes that, 'Chamberlain's and Churchill's objectives were identical. Both intended to preserve the independence of Britain and its Empire. Their methods were totally different.' It was Churchill who presented the greatest hope for peace, not Chamberlain, argues Parker. Had Winston Churchill had access to the levers of power during the 1930s instead of wandering in the political wilderness he would have concentrated upon rebuilding the 'Grand Alliance' at the centre of which would have been a staunch Anglo-French coalition, linked to Russia which, through a series of mutual defensive pacts would have opened up the possibility of a war on two fronts, giving Hitler pause for thought, particularly prior to Munich in September 1938, and thus perhaps fortifying the anti-Nazi resistance to remove him.[31] Indeed Churchill was adamant in *The Gathering Storm* that, 'there is no doubt that Hitler would have been compelled by his own General Staff to withdraw [if the French had mobilised against him in 1936]; and a check would have been given to his pretensions which might well have been fatal to his rule.' However, as John Ramsden observes in his insightful analysis of Churchill's syntax, 'note the way in which that sentence slides imperceptibly from a confident "there is no doubt" via two hopeful "would have been[s]" to a suggestive "might well have been."'[32]

For his part Chamberlain dismissed the idea of a resurrected 'Grand Alliance' in April 1938, informing the House of Commons that, in his view far from being a step towards peace, the division of Europe into rival power blocks, *would inevitably plunge us into war*. Chamberlain and the General Staff harboured severe doubts about the military capabilities and reliability of both France and Russia, a view, which in the case of France, defeated by superior strategy, was sadly vindicated by history. American isolationism, profound distrust of Stalinism and a wavering commitment from the Commonwealth, which only united behind Britain once all other options had been exhausted, also convinced Chamberlain, rightly or wrongly, that appeasement was the only course open to him. Although there is not the room to engage in counter-factual history in this slim volume, Parker's latest work amply illustrates David Dutton's observation, that 'the historiography of appeasement thus completes a some-what bizarre full circle, returning in the minds of at least some scholars very much to the point of departure in 1940'.[33]

Chapter 8: An Assessment

Chamberlain loathed war. One cannot reproach him for that. That he attempted to avert a war ardently desired by Hitler does him no discredit either. As indicated earlier, appeasement was a 'double policy' that hitched diplomacy to the deterrence of rearmament. This latter objective was an indication that Chamberlain was certainly not so confident in the certainties of peace as to ignore rearmament. Indeed Chamberlain's basic strategy was encapsulated in his comment to the Foreign Secretary, Lord Halifax: *Edward, we must hope for the best while preparing for the worst.*[1] Men like Chamberlain and Baldwin feared the consequences of modern warfare all the more because technological innovations had rendered the instruments of war even more deadly. Indeed the omnipresent fear of an aerial armada bringing death from above reverberated throughout their discussions on the subject. 'The Bomber will always get through', Stanley Baldwin had lamented to the House of Commons in the 1930s, giving rise to the spectre of Britain being powerless to stop Germany delivering a 'knock-out blow'. Chamberlain's fear was equally palpable. Flying back from his second meeting with Hitler Chamberlain remarked to Sir Horace Wilson: *You know, it is a terrible thing to be responsible for the decision as to peace or war, knowing that if it is war there is very little we can do to save these people.*[2] This dread, greatly exaggerated and never subjected to thorough analysis at the time, of the destructive potential of air was nevertheless comparable to that of limited nuclear war today. It was omnipresent in Chamberlain's fearful calculations and propelled him forwards towards ever more tenuous and discreditable efforts to purchase peace.

Given the woeful state of Britain's defences this was hardly surprising. Following the First World War Britain's chances of honouring its obligations under the terms of the Locarno Pact were bleak. As the Chiefs of Staff warned the Cabinet in June 1926: '... so far as commitments on the Continent are concerned, the services can only take note of them.' In this sense, and with Imperial defence, spearheaded by the Royal Navy, at the forefront of strategic thinking, appeasement of one kind or another was inevitable. Britain had neither the will nor resources for Continental entanglements. In tackling the question of rearmament Chamberlain was almost starting from scratch, so low had the British armed services sunk since 1919.[3] As Chancellor of the Exchequer and subsequently as Prime Minister, Chamberlain played the pivotal role in preparing the nation for war. His cautious approach to rearmament has been damned by critics, in particular those who feel he was short sighted for failing to assimilate the teachings of economist John Maynard Keynes – whose ideas are now less fashionable than when Chamberlain was being assailed for not adopting them – or because he resisted a rise in income tax to fund a defence loan. Never having time for the unorthodox approach of the former, Chamberlain dismissed the latter as *the broad road to ruin*. Chamberlain's caution is understandable. No one in government, least of all Chamberlain, expected the United States to continue its credit indefinitely and the spectre of national bankruptcy loomed large in his thinking, as did the international disarmament conference which added to his reluctance to embark on a full scale rearmament programme.[4] Omnipresent in Chamberlain's calculations was the fear that too much rearmament too soon would, *impair our stability, and our staying power in peace and war.*[5] There was of course no point of constructing a strong military machine

Edward, we must hope for the best while preparing for the worst.

CHAMBERLAIN TO HALIFAX

if the economic infrastructure supporting it collapsed at the first sign of stress. Indeed Chamberlain's essential dilemma was to reconcile, 'safety with solvency ... a task of considerable difficulty.'[6]

Chamberlain's financial prudence reflected the determination of the Treasury to control the purse strings and his thinking certainly bore the imprimatur of senior Treasury officials including Edward Bridges, Richard Hopkins and Frederick Phillips. In deciding the parameters of the defence debate it was the Treasury who were the principal agency, asserting their will with ease over the disunited service departments of which only the Air Ministry won Treasury support because its demands dovetailed with its own thinking. In essence the Treasury with Chamberlain at the helm were concerned that rearmament did not lead to massive tax rises and runaway inflation which could lead to a potential collapse in consumer spending and a rapid descent into the maelstrom of economic depression from which the country had only just emerged, the consequences of which were that 'the Government made a conscious choice to take risks with defence rather than finance.' As it had been during 1931 Chamberlain's thinking was also dictated by the demands of the City which opposed government borrowing and indeed government intervention in the economy full stop, a position to which Chamberlain (like Baldwin) was only to happy to acquiesce.[7] Whether Chamberlain's approach to the problem was correct or not it is at least fair to say that had he thrown caution to the winds and pursued a programme of rapid rearmament this in itself could have been disastrous. Chamberlain's financial 'rationing' helped Britain weather the sterling crisis in 1936 without drastically upsetting the balance of payments which would have resulted in economic turmoil and *ergo* far fewer modern fighter planes and anti-aircraft guns than were actually available in 1940.[8]

Chamberlain did not ignore rearmament, indeed he supported it against considerable public opposition, a position that only changed in 1938. In August 1935 Chamberlain had learned that Germany was borrowing £1,000 million to finance her own rearmament and that she had the industrial capacity for 'rapid expansion'. In conjunction with Baldwin he set about to *hurry our own rearmament*, envisaging spending an extra £120 million over the course of the following *four or five years*. Aware of the public hostility to rearmament, both men publicly downplayed the true level of expenditure though Chamberlain, who had urged Baldwin to make rearmament a central plank of the 1935 general election, was aware that concealment would *lay ourselves open to the more damaging accusation that we had deliberately deceived the public.* Ironically this led to the far more damaging accusation that Baldwin had placed the interests of the Conservative Party above those of the country, a criticism levelled most vehemently by Churchill.[9] In the aftermath of the 1935 general election Chamberlain appeared to confirm Churchill's charge: *when the country learns what we have spent this year on armaments over & above estimates it is going to get a shock. And it will be a good thing because it may help to prepare them for worse – much worse – to come.*[10] By 1936 Chamberlain had increased defence spending to £186 million on defence out of an overall budget of £797 million in its arms race with Germany, which Chamberlain was at pains to ensure was not interpreted as a provocative move by Hitler.[11]

Chamberlain was not yet Prime Minister, however, and the overall responsibility for the lacklustre implementation of the rearmament programme was the responsibility of Baldwin whose 'largely negative' approach meant that rearmament suffered from a profound lack of direction between 1935 and 1936. Indeed it was not until Chamberlain became Prime Minister in 1937 that any semblance of cohesion and direction was brought to the rearmament programme in an attempt to bring Britain's commitments into line with her resources, though many of underlining assumptions and assessments underpinning this drive were themselves misinformed.[12] In an attempt to stop spending on rearmament spiralling out of control Baldwin had appointed a Minister for the Co-ordination of Defence, though only after some delay, during which Churchill, who coveted the post for himself quipped that, 'Mr Baldwin is engaged in searching for a man of abilities inferior to his own. This Herculean task is of necessity occupying some time.'[13] The announcement that Sir Thomas Inskip had been appointed did little to revive confidence and was famously derided as the worst decision since Caligula made his horse a consul. Inskip, commanding physically though not politically, failed to prove his critics wrong, acting as little more than his master's voice. His defence review of December 1937 reflected Chamberlain's thinking concerning the 'rationing' as a means of reducing the nation's defensive overheads which in turn led the Chiefs of Staff amongst others to press Chamberlain for ever greater exertions to reduce Britain's overall number of potential enemies.[14] The costs of rearmament were by this point becoming *fearful*. Inskip's review initially recommended spending £1,500 million on defence over five years, increased the following year to £1,650 million with a further review in two years, much of which was spent on fighter planes and radar technology. Chamberlain was particularly concerned by the escalating cost of defence spending, necessitating additional funds if it were to be maintained at that level over any significant length of time. And well he might have been. As David Dilks has observed, it is seldom noticed that the rate of expenditure authorised in 1939 over five years was £3,000 million on aggregate, a complete abandonment of earlier financial restraints, a spending spree which to all intents and purposes was unsustainable over the long term and would have had severe consequences for Britain had the United States not intervened in the latter half of 1940.[15]

One of the key criticisms generated from the rearmament debate was directed at Chamberlain's failure to make good use of the 'breathing space' it was claimed Munich had won for Britain. Indeed Chamberlain's failure to convey any impression of dynamic activity and quell public disquiet on the matter certainly damaged his reputation. As one disgruntled Conservative MP recorded in his diary following Dunkirk '... one feels that there has been no real drive behind our war effort for the last nine months. Chamberlain will have to bear the blame for this ... He should, therefore, have resigned long ago.'[16] This lacklustre approach was reflected most graphically in the way that Chamberlain, acting more as a corporate manager than a political leader, kow-towed to the City which as long ago as 1935 had warned him and Baldwin of the perils of imposing controls on the economy, particularly since this would interfere with their profit margins. Indeed Chamberlain failed to exert, or rather actively resisted, calls to exert firm governmental control over the defence industries that could have paving the way for the effective transformation from peacetime to wartime production for fear of antagonising captains of industry, the Conservative's natural constituency. Chamberlain colluded with industry to oppose controls for fear of causing economic dislocation despite the dire military situation facing Britain.[17] Only at 'a very late stage' in 1938 did Chamberlain countenance government intervention as a means of accelerating rearmament.[18]

Chamberlain's principal concern was not to jeopardise the *fourth arm of defence* and his subsequent decision to plough Britain's meagre resources into her aerial deterrent had profound strategic ramifications for its foreign policy because it shaped the type of war that Britain could fight. Earlier all-pervasive fears of the ubiquitous bomber helped launch the primacy of aerial deterrence to the detriment of overall military preparedness. Defensive aerial deterrence failed to translate itself into a fully-rounded doctrine of deterrence which would allow Britain to fulfil her obligations under the terms of the Locarno pact because it had such 'slender means' at its disposal that any attempt to honour these commitments would in reality seriously jeopardise its Imperial commitments. It was this unpalatable choice in mind, which persuaded the Defence Requirements Committee (DRC) to advise that although Germany was now 'ultimate potential enemy' Japan remained a more immediate threat and would have to be 'pacified' – the word appeasement had not yet entered the lexicon – in order to maintain the *status quo*. Chamberlain immediately recognised that Germany was now the greatest threat to British interests in Europe but interpreted the DRC report to mean that Britain should deter not fight, subsequently moulding the nation's defences accordingly to the detriment of the army, which was woefully neglected, ruling out effective continental engagement. By February 1938 Britain's expeditionary force consisted of little more than two divisions – lightly equipped 'for an eastern theatre' – and it was not until the following February that the Cabinet decided to raise a full 'Continental' army of 32 divisions, as defensive necessity overtook financial prudence as the order of the day.[19]

Leaving the British army so poorly equipped for such a long period meant that appeasement became a self-fulfilling prophecy producing a deadening effect upon alternative diplomatic initiatives. Indeed greater concentration on land forces at an earlier stage accompanied consequently by a less timorous foreign policy would have signalled Britain's determination to honour her continental commitments, providing succour to the demoralised French and perhaps reinvigorating the international community itself leading, perhaps, to a reconstruction of the Grand Alliance advocated by Churchill. As it was Hitler interpreted this lacuna (as did Britain's demoralised French allies) that Britain had no intention of fielding a continental army and thus he had a free hand to bend Europe to his will. Britain's defence policy, which was based on deterrence, also had profound diplomatic ramifications in that it meant that Britain only belatedly felt justified in seriously seeking allies, including the Soviet Union, who could help her contain Germany. Chamberlain had opined in January 1938 that *in the absence of a powerful ally, and until our armaments are completed, we must adjust our foreign policy to our circumstances, and even bear with patience and good humour actions which we should like to treat in a very different fashion.*[20]

In the absence of a powerful ally, and until our armaments are completed, we must adjust our foreign policy to our circumstances.

CHAMBERLAIN

However, Britain's international isolation owed much to the strategy Chamberlain pursued until February 1939 when he belatedly changed course. As David Dutton has noted: 'It is reasonable to observe that Chamberlain spent much more of his time and energy trying to reduce the number of the country's enemies than he did trying to increase the number of its potential allies.'[21] Although Chamberlain was prepared to incur Hitler's displeasure at Munich by refusing to allow him a free hand in the East, his not unfounded distrust of the Soviet Union, bolstered by MI6's erroneous assessment that the Red Army 'could do nothing of real value', inhibited him from taking the logical next step, that of forging an alliance with Russia which would have acted as a check on Hitler's ambitions. Lord Strang, who took part in the Moscow negotiations in June 1939, blamed the failure of the negotiations on Polish intransigence towards Russia and their refusal to have the Red Army stationed on Polish soil, not to mention Soviet suspicion of Western motives which led ultimately to the signing of the Nazi-Soviet Pact, an easier undertaking as it required no obligation other than non-aggression and which detached Russia from any reciprocal defensive arrangement with the Allies until 1941.[22] Whatever the ultimate reason for the failure to construct a new system of collective security that included the Soviet Union, A J P Taylor lambasted the failure of the British government to conclude such a pact as 'the most incompetent transactions since Lord North lost the American colonies'.[23]

This failure to construct an alternate system of collective security also highlighted the importance of earlier failures in British diplomacy. If Britain could not afford to fight a war on three fronts – and it most assuredly could not – then Chamberlain, prompted by the Chiefs of Staff who were quite emphatic about it, set himself the task of reducing the number of enemies arrayed against Britain by trying to detach Italy from the Axis, which was keeping the Royal Navy from meeting its commitments in the Far East. Chamberlain worked desperately for a restoration of Anglo-Italian relations and his failure to achieve it, particularly when coupled with the opposition of Labour and the obduracy of Anthony Eden, who ironically, given his unwarranted reputation as an anti-appeaser was far more conciliatory towards Germany, should have reinforced in Chamberlain's mind just how diplomatically precarious and unworkable appeasement was if the dictators decided not to play ball. Eden was vehemently opposed to Mussolini who he believed to be 'a complete gangster' whilst Chamberlain, backed by the Chiefs of Staff, struggled to try and re-establish relations with the dictator in the hope of driving a wedge between him and Hitler. In this strategy Chamberlain had the ear of Count Dino Grandi, Italian Ambassador who was only too aware that Eden's hostility threatened Anglo-Italian *rapprochement* and tailored his reports to Mussolini to paint Chamberlain as 'much more of a friend and admirer than he actually was'. Eden's constant rebuffs when the *de jure* recognition of Mussolini's Abyssinian conquest was broached ultimately helped drive Mussolini into Hitler's arms. Prior to his resignation Eden and Chamberlain had a 'set-to' during which Chamberlain angrily stated: *Anthony, you have thrown away chance after chance.* It may have been Chamberlain that had missed the real window of opportunity, however. '... Had Chamberlain steeled himself to sack Eden at this time, rather than later, it is probable that Mussolini would not have been driven to ally himself with Hitler,' contends Richard Lamb.[24] Whatever the outcome may have been, had Chamberlain been able to forge a genuine Anglo-Italian alliance, however unpalatable this idea appears today, the reality was that the Eden's resignation removed the last obstacle from Chamberlain's personal control of British foreign policy and accelerated appeasement,

One of the most enduring myths concerning Chamberlain's ill-fated premiership was that a secret cabal of close advisers, headed by his *eminence grise* Sir Horace Wilson, actually conspired to withhold information from Chamberlain which indicated that Hitler could not be appeased. It was a myth propagated first and foremost by Churchill for whom the twilight world of secret intelligence held an almost lurid fascination. Seeking to exonerate the intelligence services for failing to predict the German invasion of Prague and the Italian invasion of Albania, both of which had apparently come without warning, Churchill asked the House of Commons to consider '... whether there is not some hand which intervenes and filters down or withholds intelligence from Ministers.' The hand of which he spoke was Wilson's. It was not true. Nor is it fair to say that Chamberlain wilfully ignored the Foreign Office's views. Recent research has shown that despite a torrent of retrospective post-war justifications by several diplomats who were seeking to vindicate their position, the difference between the Foreign Office and Chamberlain on matters concerning how to deal with Hitler was one largely of degree rather than substance.[25] However, Chamberlain's personal assumption of responsibility for the direction of foreign affairs in 1937 rapidly superseded the 'old diplomacy' of the Foreign Office, which had striven to maintain Britain's 'permanent interests' abroad by maintaining the balance of power in Europe. In place of the cold calculation of the Foreign Office's amoral *Realpolitik*, Chamberlain's sense of personal mission led him to chase a series of 'elusive compromises' that damaged British imperial interests and elicited little of concrete value in return except national humiliation and personal obloquy.[26] That he did so was partially because of the unrealistic utopian premise driving Chamberlain's vision of appeasement which, in the words of his close confidant Sir Horace Wilson, 'was never designed just to postpone war, or enable us to enter war more united. The aim of our appeasement was to avoid war altogether.'[27]

In seeking to achieve this halcyon end Chamberlain may not have ignored information but his decisions could only ever as good as the information upon which they were based and on which he acted in good faith. Chamberlain certainly understood the value of secret intelligence, schooled by his close friend Sir Joseph Ball, a former MI5 officer. It was during Chamberlain's premiership that Admiral Hugh 'Quex' Sinclair, the head of MI6, moved to become a key 'policy adviser'.[28] Foremost amongst the manifest shortcomings and failures of British intelligence during this crucial period was its failure to provide a balanced assessment of German strengths and weaknesses which led to a 'blindness' that generated worst-case scenarios and pessimistic predictions that gave substance to Chamberlain's innermost fears. A case in point is Czechoslovakia, which in Chamberlain's imperious phraseology was, *a quarrel in a faraway country between people of whom we know nothing*. However, the calculations that led to Munich were not simply conjured up by Chamberlain to suit his own convictions. They were based on an overwhelmingly negative appraisal of the situation derived from a range of sources including the towering figure of Sir Maurice Hankey, the Cabinet Secretary, and the Chiefs of Staff who presented Chamberlain with a counsel of despair indicating that a guarantee to Czechoslovakia would in all probability spark not just 'a limited European war only, but a world war'.[29] Under such circumstances Foreign Office mandarin Sir Alexander Cadogan advised that 'we *must* not precipitate a conflict now – we shall be smashed.'[30] Given such an unconscionably bleak scenario the head of MI6 meanwhile strongly advised that the Czechs accept 'the inevitable' and surrender the Sudetenland to Hitler. They were to be left in no uncertain terms that 'they stand alone if they refuse to recognise such a solution'.[31] Given such learned counsel Chamberlain believed he had no alternative but to seek a settlement with Hitler. To do otherwise would be to provide a pretext for a war that Britain's political and military planners did not want.

The Chiefs of Staff were undoubtedly correct in their assessment that the Czech army could not resist the *Wehrmacht* but its pessimistic prognosis failed to make the conceptual leap based on the fact that the Czech army's 30 divisions faced Germany's 37, whilst Britain had only two. Although such counter-factual speculation lacks any empirical foundation it is instructive to ponder Graham Stewart's conjecture that had Germany invaded Czechoslovakia in September 1938 it would have proved a far costlier excursion than its invasion of Poland the following year, perhaps giving Hitler pause for thought. A concentrated armed incursion into Czechoslovakia would have also left Germany's western flank with France dangerously exposed, defended by only eight divisions compared with France's 56. Had the French General Staff considered such an eventuality, which it did not, in conjunction with Britain, they could have driven into the heart of the Ruhr, delivering a knockout blow to a dangerously overstretched Hitler. Also lost at Munich was the sprawling Skoda armaments works whose output equalled Britain's combined armaments output and conversely was a considerable boon to the Nazis. That Chamberlain did not gamble on fighting a war in September 1938 is hardly surprising given the 'percussion of pessimism' he was subjected to by his Chiefs of Staff regarding Germany superiority and British inadequacy and which concluded on 27 September, the day before he flew to Bad Godesberg, that the 'balance of advantage is definitely in favour of postponement'.[32] The following day a trusted informant told MI5 that if Britain declared war over Czechoslovakia Hitler would order an air attack on London, confirming Chamberlain's worst fears.[33] On his return from

Bad Godesberg Chamberlain articulated the Chief of Staff's concern to Cabinet, together with emotive personal embellishment, that whilst flying over London he, 'had asked himself what degree of protection we could afford to the thousands of homes which he had seen stretched up below him, and he had felt that we were in no position to justify waging a war today in order to prevent a war hereafter.'[34]

Given the dire predictions Chamberlain received, it was logical that he chose to invest Britain's limited resources into the most cost effective deterrent on offer, the RAF. Here again, however, the failure to gain accurate information concerning the scale and rapidity of German rearmament, particularly with regard to the development of the *Luftwaffe*, was thrown into relief in March 1935 when Hitler announced that Germany had 'reached parity' with the RAF. It was not true (yet) but the panic it induced can be deduced from Sir John Simon's solemn minute to Chamberlain:

'One may have considerable doubts whether once left behind by Germany in the air we shall ever be able to attain a level of parity with her again. The conclusion which might have to be drawn … is that this country is seriously open to the threat of sudden attack by a Continental Power, in a degree to which it has not been exposed for hundreds of years.'[35]

Not only did Hitler's announcement highlight the paucity of Britain's long-range intelligence predictions, it also induced diplomatic paralysis.[36] The result of this failure should have give Chamberlain pause for thought because the incident indicated deterrence was not working and that maybe the fundamental strategies underpinning appeasement required a radical rethink. To be fair to Chamberlain defence policy belatedly received an overhaul in 1938 when, contrary to the advice of the air staff, Chamberlain pushed through a reorientation of the RAF from the deterrent of the bomber to defensive capabilities of the fighter plane.[37] In David Dilks' judgement, had Britain appreciated the enormity of the peril facing the country its rearmament programme might have been carried through earlier and with considerably more vigour, certainly several years earlier than 1936, thus avoiding such a rude awakening.[38]

That British intelligence failed during this period is hardly surprising. Since the 1920s it had been under-funded, under-manned and inexperienced, though one of the most egregious flaws was systemic: the intelligence apparatus itself. Intelligence-sharing between the Chiefs of Staffs of the three service departments was almost non-existent, each developing its own estimates and analysis of German intentions. Even the foundation of the Joint Intelligence Committee in 1936 failed to provide the British government with a cogent interpretative clearinghouse for the intelligence with which it was deluged. 'A stream of intelligence flowed into Whitehall varying from excellent to dreadful – and Whitehall found it impossible to tell the difference.' As a result the government failed to make 'sensible use' of intelligence reports like those of the Industrial Intelligence Centre regarding the levels of German industrial mobilisation, which did not circulate at a high enough level to make any impact on policy initially, but also frequently contradicting 'firm expectations' regarding the equal footing Britain believed it enjoyed with Germany on this score. This is an important point. The reception of intelligence, observed one seasoned intelligence historian, is shaped primarily by the expectations of policy makers and military strategists about what *should* happen. Intelligence warnings during the inter-war period, often ambiguous or vacillating, were frequently shaped to fit prevailing notions, stimulating self-deception rather than resolution regarding the rapidly changing realities in the balance of European power.[39]

Taking the long view of Chamberlain's historical reputation it is clear that he certainly deserves some measure of rehabilitation for his domestic record. Chamberlain was one of the most politically astute administrators operating during the inter-war period by a considerable stretch of the imagination. From Stuart Ball's research on the formation of the National Government in 1931 Chamberlain emerges not as the Machiavellian mastermind of Labour's misfortune but as a rather reluctant exponent of a 'national' government, which he accepted initially as only a short term expedient for the sake of the country. Thereafter, his stewardship at the Treasury was 'stern and grim' in the words of *The Times*, but his austere financial reconstruction, though painful, particularly as it rested on the miserly preoccupation that the poorest sections of society shoulder a disproportionate share of the burden for the financial mismanagement of the economy by the most privileged, did ultimately help restore economic confidence at a time when Britain's debt to the United States and the very real possibility of defaulting on its loan repayments would have seriously damaged Britain's international reputation.[40] Thus Chamberlain's restoration of financial stability and sincere sponsorship of a raft of progressive social legislation was an admirable record of achievement and perhaps the apogee of his political career. However, no matter what the merits for rehabilitating Chamberlain's domestic record it remains indisputable that his past achievements as a social reformer have quite literally been consigned to history whilst the question of his reputation, based on his international record, remains very much a live issue, hotly debated and fiercely contested. It is ironic that this is so. At his core

Chamberlain was not interested in foreign affairs, particularly when these involved frittering away scarce national resources, which he adamantly believed would be better spent on domestic reform rather than the construction of the weapons of war, the thought of which *is hateful and damnable.*[41]

The opening of the archives, particularly those of the Treasury, has refuted much of *Guilty Men*'s simplistic thesis particularly with regards to rearmament and the financial complexities with which Chamberlain and his minions wrestled. Indeed, given the constraints placed upon Chamberlain and his colleagues by external circumstance and the limits of their own imaginations their achievements were little short of remarkable. Graham Stewart has argued that although the RAF of 1939 was ten times stronger than it had been in September 1938 Munich, 'bought time for the RAF to win the Battle of Britain and to limit the destruction unleashed by the blitz but had the conflict come in 1938 it would probably not have been necessary to fight an aerial war over Britain in the first place.'[42] There is of course no way of proving or disproving this thesis. The fact is Britain did not fall in 1940 and it would be grossly unfair to deny Chamberlain's contribution to the astounding strides made by the RAF. Here there is certainly cause for congratulation. Churchill without doubt thought so. On 15 August 1940, having watched the deployment of the RAF against the incoming *Luftwaffe* from the headquarters of Fighter Command, Churchill's first thought on returning to Downing Street was to instruct his private secretary, 'Telephone Neville Chamberlain and give him the good news.' Chamberlain had to perform an unenviable balancing-act with the nation's finances in order to rearm but as Churchill's grateful words show to say that Chamberlain ignored rearmament is simply untenable. One always has to be careful of historical grandstanding by politicians whose memoranda can sometimes be drafted with an eye on their posthumous reputations. Churchill was a prime example of this but Chamberlain was not immune either. Following the invasion of Poland Chamberlain wrote of the devastating potential of air power to paralyse land forces, in the process vindicating his decision to give the RAF priority because, as he conceded, *I thought I must get something on record too which would have to be quoted in the Book.*[43] This might appear cynical but given the subsequent denigration of his career it was perhaps more prudent than he knew at the time. Chamberlain's pivotal role in ensuring that the RAF was able to deliver Britain's 'finest hour' has been unjustly forgotten.

These words for the defence aside, though the shifting sands of history may decide otherwise, from this vantage point, nearly 70 years after his death, it appears unlikely that any amount of ink spilled by historians will ever remove the disfiguring stain of 'appeasement' from Chamberlain's reputation. It has left an indelible mark. The irony of Chamberlain's hubristic belief that he had won *peace in our time* at Munich has overshadowed everything else he achieved. He is remembered in popular consciousness not as the revered statesman who enacted so countless pieces of progressive pieces of legislation but as a faintly ridiculous and frequently sinister figure, supping with the devil with perhaps too short a spoon. The policy with which he personally identified himself – 'appeasement' – has never become a sympathetic lamentation for one man's doomed search for peace but rather it has entered our lexicon as a term of abuse, forever synonymous with craven capitulation to the horrors of racial barbarism, bestial sadism and industrialised genocide on an unparalleled scale, an abject surrender to man's basest instincts. Chamberlain's international policies were many things but in the face of such tyranny they were hardly morally courageous or heroic, and in hindsight appeared weak at precisely the time when 'the nation' wished to project an image of strength. Chamberlain's reputation undoubtedly suffers from comparison to the Herculean figure of his successor Winston Churchill, whose victory over Nazism and Fascism – the ideologies that defeated Chamberlain's best efforts – continues to dominate national self-mythology. Chamberlain chose conciliation. Churchill opted for resistance. This unfortunate juxtaposition, which certainly glosses over the complexities of the situation, thanks in large part of Churchill's own histories of the period, goes some way to explain why popular consciousness continues to hold Chamberlain in such opprobrium.

As was noted at the outset of this chapter, a concentration on the last three years of Chamberlain's political life has distorted his historical legacy, though given the criterion for evaluating this tumultuous period this is hardly surprising. In delivering a verdict on Chamberlain's historical career whatever the mitigating circumstances one can offer in defence of his policies and judgements it is impossible for the historian to escape one incontrovertible historical fact: Chamberlain's principal policy utterly failed in almost every respect. Appeasement failed to preserve the British Empire, failed to preserve British economic stability and most obviously failed to prevent war. Projecting into the post-war period it also failed to secure electoral victory for the Conservative Party which was split by its malodorous legacy for a generation. Chamberlain was not the progenitor of appeasement but he was certainly its most enthusiastic exponent pursuing the policy more energetically than most. Contrary to popular belief appeasement was never pursuit of 'peace at any price'. It was a complex and dangerous diplomatic high-wire act, a war of nerves. As the Permanent-Under Secretary at the Foreign Office expressed it in the summer of 1939, it was necessary to steer the middle ground between provocation and the impression of weakness. 'If you are too bellicose, you provoke the Dictators into doing something irrevocable. If you are too passive, you encourage them to think they can do anything.'[44] There is little doubt that Chamberlain (and more so Baldwin) erred too far towards passivity, a tendency lampooned in the ditty: 'If at first you can't concede – Fly, fly, fly again.'[45] Chamberlain did not pursue 'peace at any price' but he consciously 'gave persuasion priority over coercion'.[46]

That he did was largely a situation of his own making. His stewardship of rearmament, though responsible for stabilising the *fourth arm of defence* and for delivering the successes of the RAF in the summer of 1940 also put British military and foreign policy on a distinct trajectory in which appeasement was the only option. The financial denigration of the British army, whilst understandable given the parameters of the defence debate during the early 1930s, meant that Britain was unable to project the power of her Empire onto the continent. Instead she retreated into the doctrines of deterrence and isolationism rather than embracing positive engagement with similarly beleaguered countries. It was this failure to explore alternative collective security arrangements until it was almost too late coupled with the direction rearmament was taking that meant that the appeasement became a self-fulfilling prophecy with unremittingly bleak advice emanating from almost every quarter reinforcing Chamberlain's own inner conviction that appeasement was the only course of action. From this position he was unmovable and it was only late in the day that he foresaw the need to change course. In fact for all its grandiose objectives all it achieved in effect was to serve as a diplomatic veneer through which to reward aggression and illegality, a process of vacillation and weakness that had begun with Manchuria in 1932 and

Abyssinia in 1935 and did not end even after Munich in 1938. Indeed far from appeasing the dictators and securing peace appeasement merely served as a green light for further acts of naked aggression.

Given the political and emotional investment Chamberlain placed in the Munich agreement it is perhaps unsurprising that he allowed himself to believe that that he had won a lasting peace. Chamberlain always refused to accept that war was *inevitable*. His sense of destiny, no less acute than that felt by his successor precluded this. Chamberlain believed in appeasement with an fervent messianic zeal indicated in his phrase *I know that I can save this country and I do not believe that anyone else can*. Moving beyond achievable *Realpolitik* Chamberlain's reliance on personal shuttle-diplomacy appears to have stimulated his belief that he alone was capable of calming the raging political passions that threatened to plunge the world into total war, a belief that militated against more sober contemplation of the realities of Nazism. Chamberlain was not so much hoodwinked by Hitler as by himself. In this sense Chamberlain was the harbinger of his own national and personal misfortune. His inability to concede that war might be inevitable, coupled with his failure to conceive that Hitler was perfectly capable of launching an unprovoked war of aggression against his neighbours, led to 'strategic blindness' fed by his own vanity, arrogance and personal aloofness, which enabled him to delude himself that his opinions carried some weight with Hitler. This failure to understand that the dictators were operating outside the rules of diplomatic engagement highlighted perhaps the most egregious flaw in the strategy of appeasement. Perhaps Chamberlain understood otherwise. After all he 'could hardly have come back from Munich and told the House of Commons that he had talked to Hitler but he did not believe a word Hitler had said and that he thought war would come, as this could have precipitated the very thing he was trying to avoid'.[47] The weight of historical evidence suggests otherwise, however. This was Chamberlain's greatest error of judgement. Owing to his short-term analysis of the Czechoslovakian crisis and his inability to conceive of the genuine nature of Nazism, Chamberlain could not have been more misguided in his fanciful notion Hitler had been sated. The scale of his monstrous appetite was greater than Chamberlain could have ever imagined. Yet as his diaries and letters indicate as far as Chamberlain was concerned one of the fringe benefits of Munich was that it afforded him a moral insurance policy. If Hitler chose to contravene the terms of the Munich agreement it would show the world, and particularly the Americans not to mention subsequent generations that it was Hitler who was acting in bad faith and not the British.

Despite this precaution Hitler easily massaged Chamberlain's increasing sense of self-righteousness and excessive vanity and he allowed him to believe that he had not only secured peace but also built a lasting rapport with the dictator who respected him as a statesman. This was simply not the case Hitler regarded those who had capitulated to him at Munich as 'worms' and would not be bought off with diplomacy again. It was not Hitler who had *missed the bus* at Munich but Chamberlain who must have felt bitterly contrite when British intelligence intercepted several messages replete with disparaging references to him soon after Munich. And yet still the pantomime of self-deception rolled on into the following year, even after the rape of Prague, with Chamberlain's guarantee to Poland (who had not been backwards in coming forward to help Hitler dismember Czechoslovakia). This was no line in the sand as commonly conceived. Chamberlain guaranteed Polish 'independence' not its territorial integrity, a decision designed to provide leeway for nego-tiating further concessions with Hitler regarding a Polish corridor. Ultimately this was perhaps Chamberlain's greatest folly, to continue believing in the chimera of appeasement long after even its most hardened proponent had realised that military action against Hitler was both imminent and necessary.

NOTES

Prologue: Chamberlain's character, outlook and image

1. Arthur Salter, *Slave of the Lamp: A Public Servant's Notebook* (Weidenfeld and Nicholson, London: 1967) p 142.

2. Robert Self (ed), *The Neville Chamberlain Diary Letters, Vol. 1: The Making of a Politician, 1915–1920* (Ashgate, Aldershot: 2000) p 6, hereafter *NCDL Vol. 1*.

3. Charles Petrie, *The Chamberlain Tradition* (Right Book Club, London: 1938) p 224.

4. Cyril Clemens, *The Man from Limehouse: Clement Richard Attlee* (Didier, New York: 1946) p 39.

5. A J P Taylor, *English History 1914–1945* (Oxford University Press, London: 1965) p 256.

6. Alistair Horne, *Harold Macmillan: Volume One* (Macmillan, London: 1988) p 115.

7. Francis Williams, *A Pattern of Rulers* (Longmans, London: 1965) p 135.

8. N J Crowson (ed), *Fleet Street, Press Barons and Politics: The Journals of Collin Brooks, 1932–1940* (Royal Historical Society/UCL, London: 1998) p 278.

9. Richard Cockett (ed), *My Dear Max: The Letters of Brendan Bracken to Lord Beaverbrook, 1925–1958* (Historians Press, London: 1990) p 45.

10. Salter, *Slave of the Lamp*, p 172.

11. Petrie, *The Chamberlain Tradition*, p 213.

12. Lord Templewood, *Nine Troubled Years* (Collins, London: 1934) p 388.

13. Lord Vansittart, *The Mist Procession* (Hutchinson, London: 1958) pp 429–30.

14. John Colville, *The Fringes of Power* (Hodder and Stoughton, London: 1985) pp 35–6.

15. Graham Stewart, *Burying Caesar: The Churchill-Chamberlain Rivalry* (Overlook Press, New York: 2001) p 137.

16. R A Butler, *The Art of the Possible: The Memoirs of Lord Butler* (Hamish Hamilton, London: 1971) p 78.

17. Stewart, *Burying Caesar*, p 47.

18. Neville Chamberlain to Hilda Chamberlain, 5 March 1939, in Robert Self (ed), *The Neville Chamberlain Diary Letters, Vol. 4* (Ashgate, Aldershot: 2005) p 390, hereafter *NCDL, Vol. 4*.

19. Butler, *The Art of the Possible*, pp 78–9.

20. Stuart Ball (ed), *Parliament and Politics in the Age of MacDonald and Baldwin: The Headlam Diaries* (Historians Press, London: 1992) pp 112–13.

21. Lord Vansittart, *The Mist Procession*, pp 429–30.

22. Robert Rhodes James (ed), *Memoirs of a Conservative: J.C.C. Davidson's Memoirs and Papers, 1910–37* (Weidenfeld and Nicolson, London: 1969) pp 418 and 381.

23. Ball (ed), *Parliament and Politics in the Age of Churchill and Attlee*, p 87.

24. *The Times*, 11 November 1940.

25. Austen Chamberlain to Ida Chamberlain, 2 November 1924 in Robert Self (ed.), *The Austen Chamberlain Diary Letters* (Royal Historical Society/CUP, Cambridge: 1995) p 259.

26. John Harvey (ed), *The Diplomatic Diaries of Oliver Harvey, 1937–1940* (Collins, London: 1970) p 233.

27. Lord Citrine, *Men and Work: An Autobiography* (Hutchinson, London: 1964) p 368.
28. Keith Middlemas and John Barnes, *Baldwin: A Biography* (Weidenfeld and Nicolson, London: 1969) p 1046.
29. Neville Chamberlain to Ida Chamberlain, 17 December 1938 in *NCDL, Vol. 4*, p 370.
30. Neville Chamberlain to Ida Chamberlain, 16 February 1935 in *NCDL, Vol. 4*, p 116.
31. Neville Chamberlain to Hilda Chamberlain, 15 October 1935 in *NCDL, Vol. 4*, p 156.
32. Neville Chamberlain to Hilda Chamberlain, 26 June 1937 in *NCDL, Vol. 4*, p 256.
33. Neville Chamberlain to Ida Chamberlain, 16 February 1936 in *NCDL, Vol. 4*, p 178.
34. Neville Chamberlain to Hilda Chamberlain, 10 April 1937 in *NCDL, Vol. 4*, p 245.
35. Neville Chamberlain to Ida Chamberlain, 20 June 1937 in *NCDL, Vol. 4*, p 255.
36. Neville Chamberlain to Hilda Chamberlain, 13 March 1937 and Neville Chamberlain to Ida Chamberlain, 20 June 1937 in *NCDL, Vol. 4*, pp 241 and 255.
37. Neville Chamberlain to Hilda Chamberlain, 23 March 1935 in *NCDL, Vol. 4*, p 123.
38. Neville Chamberlain to Hilda Chamberlain, 15 October 1939 in *NCDL, Vol. 4*, p 459.

Chapter 1: Early Life

1. David Dilks, *Neville Chamberlain* Vol. 1 (Cambridge University Press, Cambridge: 1984), p 86.
2. Keith Feiling, *The Life of Neville Chamberlain* (Macmillan: London 1946) p 27.
3. Feiling, *The Life of Neville Chamberlain*, p 29.

4. Feiling, *The Life of Neville Chamberlain*, p 31.
5. Feiling, *The Life of Neville Chamberlain*, p 38.
6. Feiling, *The Life of Neville Chamberlain*, p 39.
7. Iain MacLeod, *Neville Chamberlain* (Frederick Muller, London: 1961) pp 39–40.
8. Feiling, *The Life of Neville Chamberlain*, p 33.
9. Feiling, *The Life of Neville Chamberlain*, p 46.
10. Keith Feiling, *The Life of Neville Chamberlain*, p 51.
11. John Ramsden, *The Age of Balfour and Baldwin, 1902–1940* (Longman, London: 1978) p 356.
12. Neville Chamberlain to Hilda Chamberlain, 17 September 1939 in *NCDL, Vol. 4*, p 449.

Chapter 2: Westminster, Birmingham and Back

1. Austen Chamberlain to Hilda Chamberlain, 21 December 1916 in Robert Self (ed), *The Austen Chamberlain Diary Letters*, p 37.
2. Kevin O Morgan (ed), *Lloyd George: Family Letters, 1885–1936* (Oxford University Press, Oxford: 1973) p 185.
3. Charles Petrie, *The Chamberlain Tradition*, p 223.
4. Phillip Williamson (ed), *The Modernisation of Conservative Politics: The Diaries and Letters of William Bridgeman, 1904–1935* (Historian's Press, London: 1988) p 125.
5. Austen Chamberlain to Ida Chamberlain, 15 February 1918 in Robert Self (ed), *The Austen Chamberlain Diary Letters*, p 73
6. Ramsden, *The Age of Balfour and Baldwin*, p 136.
7. David Lloyd George, *War Memoirs: Vol. 3* (Odhams Press, London: 1934) p 1368.

8. Austen Chamberlain to Ida Chamberlain, 19 January 1935 in Robert Self (ed), *The Austen Chamberlain Diary Letters*, p 473.

9. Neville Chamberlain to Ida Chamberlain, 9 February 1918 and Neville Chamberlain to Hilda Chamberlain, 23 February 1918 in *NCDL, Vol. 1*, pp 254 and 256.

10. Feiling, *The Life of Neville Chamberlain*, p 76.

11. Quoted in David Dutton, *Neville Chamberlain* (Arnold, London: 2001), p 11.

12. Neville Chamberlain to Hilda Chamberlain, 4 January 1919 in *NCDL, Vol. 1*, p 304.

13. Robert Skidelsky, *Oswald Mosley* (Papermac, London: 1990) pp 131–2.

14. Skidelsky, *Oswald Mosley*, pp 131–2.

15. Ramsden, *The Age of Balfour and Baldwin*, pp 195, 267, 271 and 291.

16. Stewart, *Burying Caesar*, p 37.

17. Neville Chamberlain to Ida Chamberlain, 26 July 1930, in *NCDL, Vol. 3*, p 200.

18. Neville Chamberlain to Hilda Chamberlain, 4 August 1930 in *NCDL, Vol. 3*, p 203.

19. Robert Self, 'Introduction', *NCDL, Vol. 3*, p 15.

20. Rhodes James (ed), *Memoirs of a Conservative*, pp 342–3.

21. Ball (ed), *Parliament and Politics in the Age of MacDonald and Baldwin*, p 203.

22. Neville Chamberlain to Hilda Chamberlain, 16 August 1931 in *NCDL, Vol. 3*, p 274.

23. Stuart Ball, 'The Conservative Party and the Formation of the National Government: August 1931', *The Historical Journal*, 29, 1 (1986) pp 159–82.

24. Feiling, *The Life of Neville Chamberlain*, p 193.

25. Ball, 'The Conservative Party and the Formation of the National Government', pp 159–82.

26. John Ramsden, *An Appetite for Power* (Harper Collins, London: 1998) p 280.
27. Ball, 'The Conservative Party and the Formation of the National Government: August 1931', pp 159–82.

Chapter 3: Backbone of the Government

1. Ramsden, *The Age of Balfour and Baldwin*, p 338.
2. Stewart, *Burying Caesar*, p 118.
3. Stewart, *Burying Caesar*, pp 122–5.
4. David Dutton, *Neville Chamberlain* (Arnold, London: 2001) p 17.
5. Neville Chamberlain to Ida Chamberlain, 9 June 1934 in *NCDL, Vol. 4*, p 73.
6. Neville Chamberlain to Hilda Chamberlain, 28 November 1936 and Neville Chamberlain to Ida Chamberlain, 8 December 1936 in *NCDL, Vol. 4*, pp 225–6.
7. Neville Chamberlain to Ida Chamberlain, 12 May 1934 in *NCDL, Vol. 4*, p 70.
8. Neville Chamberlain to Ida Chamberlain, 9 June 1934 in *NCDL, Vol. 4*, p 73.
9. Neville Chamberlain to Hilda Chamberlain, 23 March 1935 in *NCDL, Vol. 4*, p 125.
10. Martin Gilbert, *Winston S. Churchill, Vol. V, 1922–1939* (Heinemann, London: 1976) p 455.
11. MacLeod, *Neville Chamberlain*, p 178.
12. Stewart, *Burying Caesar*, pp 210–11.
13. *Hansard*, Vol. 292, HC Debs, col 2339, 30 July 1934.
14. MacLeod, *Neville Chamberlain*, p 178.
15. Stewart, *Burying Caesar*, p 213.
16. Neville Chamberlain to Ida Chamberlain, 28 July 1934 in *NCDL, Vol. 4*, pp 82–3.
17. Stewart, *Burying Caesar*, pp 211 and 214.

18. Neville Chamberlain to Ida Chamberlain, 4 August 1934 in *NCDL, Vol. 4*, p 85.
19. Neville Chamberlain to Ida Chamberlain, 8 December 1935 in *NCDL, Vol. 4*, p 165.
20. Neville Chamberlain to Hilda Chamberlain, 9 March 1935 in *NCDL, Vol. 4*, p 119.
21. MacLeod, *Neville Chamberlain*, p 178.
22. Neville Chamberlain to Hilda Chamberlain, 30 March 1935 in *NCDL, Vol. 4*, p 125.
23. Michael Howard, 'British Military Preparations for the Second World War', in David Dilks (ed), *Retreat From Power: Studies in Britain's Foreign Policy of the Twentieth Century, Vol. One, 1906–1939* (Macmillan, London: 1981) pp 102–3.
24. Neville Chamberlain to Ida Chamberlain, 28 July 1934 in *NCDL, Vol. 4*, pp 82–3.
25. R A C Parker, *Chamberlain and Appeasement* (Macmillan, London: 1993) pp 32–3.
26. Neville Chamberlain to Hilda Chamberlain, 12 May 1935 in *NCDL, Vol. 4*, p 133.
27. Neville Chamberlain to Ida Chamberlain, 14 March 1936 in *NCDL, Vol. 4*, p 179.
28. Neville Chamberlain to Hilda Chamberlain, 9 February 1936 in *NCDL, Vol. 4*, p 175.
29. Neville Chamberlain to Ida Chamberlain, 29 February 1936 in *NCDL, Vol. 4*, p 178.
30. Neville Chamberlain to Hilda Chamberlain, 28 November 1936 in *NCDL, Vol. 4*, p 224.
31. Stewart, *Burying Caesar*, pp 223–4.
32. Parker, *Chamberlain and Appeasement*, p 276.
33. Neville Chamberlain to Hilda Chamberlain, 25 April1937 in *NCDL, Vol. 4*, pp 246–8.

34. Neville Chamberlain to Ida Chamberlain, 7 March 1937 in *NCDL, Vol. 4*, p 239.
35. Neville Chamberlain to Ida and Hilda Chamberlain, 9 December 1934 in *NCDL, Vol. 4*, p 104.
36. Middlemas and Barnes, *Baldwin: A Biography*, p 590.
37. Neville Chamberlain to Hilda Chamberlain, 22 May 1935 in *NCDL, Vol. 4*, p 136.
38. Neville Chamberlain to Hilda Chamberlain, 10 November 1935 in *NCDL, Vol. 4*, pp 82–3.
39. Neville Chamberlain to Ida Chamberlain, 8 December 1935 in *NCDL, Vol. 4*, p 165.
40. Neville Chamberlain to Ida Chamberlain, 28 March 1936 and 13 April 1936 in *NCDL, Vol. 4*, p 182.
41. Neville Chamberlain to Hilda Chamberlain, 6 September 1936 in *NCDL, Vol. 4*, p 207.
42. Neville Chamberlain to Hilda Chamberlain, 14 November 1936 in *NCDL, Vol. 4*, p 220.
43. Neville Chamberlain to Hilda Chamberlain, 13 December 1936 in *NCDL, Vol. 4*, pp 227–9.
44. Neville Chamberlain to Hilda Chamberlain, 13 December 1936 in *NCDL, Vol. 4*, p 229.
45. Lord Blake, *The Conservative Party from Peel to Major* (Heinemann, London: 1997) p 238.
46. Neville Chamberlain to Ida Chamberlain, 21 March 1937 in *NCDL, Vol. 4*, p 242.

Chapter 4: Prime Minister

1. Neville Chamberlain to Hilda Chamberlain, 30 May 1937 in *NCDL, Vol. 4*, p 253.
2. Ramsden, *The Age of Balfour and Baldwin*, p 355.
3. Neville Chamberlain to Hilda Chamberlain, 30 May 1937 in *NCDL, Vol. 4*, p 253.

4. Lord Templewood, *Nine Troubled Years* (Collins, London: 1954) p 388.

5. Neville Chamberlain to Ida Chamberlain, 16 October 1937 in *NCDL, Vol. 4*, p 275.

6. Earl Swinton, *Sixty Years of Power: Some Memories of the Men who wielded it* (Hutchinson, London: 1966) pp 111, 114.

7. Viscount Simon, *Retrospect* (Hutchinson, London: 1952) p 278.

8. Parker, *Chamberlain and Appeasement*, p 94.

9. Herbert Samuel, *Memoirs* (Cressett Press, London: 1945) p 215.

10. Ian Colvin, *The Chamberlain Cabinet* (Gollancz, London: 1971) pp 261–2.

11. Neville Chamberlain to Hilda Chamberlain, 27 March 1938 in *NCDL, Vol. 4*, p 311.

12. Ian Colvin, *The Chamberlain Cabinet*, p 263.

13. Lord Templewood, *Nine Troubled Years*, p 388.

14. Sidney Aster, ' "Guilty Men": The Case of Neville Chamberlain' in Robert Boyce and Esmonde M Robertson (eds), *Paths to War: New Essays on the Origins of the Second World War* (St Martins Press, London: 1989) pp 241–3.

15. Neville Chamberlain to Hilda Chamberlain, 25 June 1938 in *NCDL, Vol. 4*, p 330.

16. Ramsden, *The Age of Balfour and Baldwin*, p 357.

17. Neville Chamberlain to Ida Chamberlain, 9 October 1938 in *NCDL, Vol. 4*, p 353.

18. Neville Chamberlain to Ida Chamberlain, 13 March 1939 in *NCDL, Vol. 4*, p 391.

19. Lord Vansittart, *The Mist Procession*, p 430.

20. Anthony Eden, *Facing the Dictators* (Cassell, London: 1962), p 445.

21. John Harvey (ed), *The Diplomatic Diaries of Oliver Harvey, 1937–1940* (Collins, London: 1970) p 27.

22. R J Minney, *The Private Papers of Hore-Belisha* (Collins, London: 1960) p 16.

23. Ball (ed), *Parliament and Politics in the Age of Churchill and Attlee*, p 111.

24. Dutton, *Neville Chamberlain*, pp 17–18.

25. Neville Chamberlain to Ida Chamberlain, 17 November 1934 in *NCDL, Vol. 4*, p 101.

26. MacLeod, *Neville Chamberlain*, p 179.

27. Dutton, *Neville Chamberlain*, p 205.

28. Neville Chamberlain to Hilda Chamberlain, 28 July 1934 in *NCDL, Vol. 4*, p 80.

29. Neville Chamberlain to Hilda Chamberlain, 30 July 1939 in *NCDL, Vol. 4*, pp 333–4.

30. Neville Chamberlain to Hilda Chamberlain, 18 March 1935 in *NCDL, Vol. 4*, p 123.

31. Neville Chamberlain to Hilda Chamberlain, 29 August 1937 in *NCDL, Vol. 4*, p 267.

32. David Dutton, *Anthony Eden: A Life and Reputation* (Arnold, London: 1997) p 73; and Neville Chamberlain to Hilda Chamberlain, 14 June 1936 in *NCDL, Vol. 4*, p 194.

33. Daniel Waley, *British Public Opinion and the Abyssinian War, 1935–6* (Maurice Temple Smith/LSE, London: 1975) pp 44–71.

34. Neville Chamberlain to Hilda Chamberlain, 28 November 1936 in *NCDL, Vol. 4*, p 224.

35. Neville Chamberlain to Ida Chamberlain, 4 July1937 in *NCDL, Vol. 4*, p 259.

36. Neville Chamberlain to Hilda Chamberlain, 1 August 1937 in *NCDL, Vol. 4*, p 264.

37. Feiling, *The Life of Neville Chamberlain*, p 330.

38. Neville Chamberlain to Ida Chamberlain, 8 August 1937 in *NCDL, Vol. 4*, p 265.

39. Neville Chamberlain to Hilda Chamberlain, 29 August 1937 in *NCDL, Vol. 4*, p 267.

40. Neville Chamberlain to Hilda Chamberlain, 12 September 1937 in *NCDL, Vol. 4*, p 270.

41. Andrew J Crozier, *Appeasement and Germany's Last Bid for Colonies* (Macmillan, London: 1988) p 205.

42. Richard Lamb, *Mussolini and the British* (John Murray, London: 1997) p 191.

43. Neville Chamberlain to Ida Chamberlain, 26 November 1937 in *NCDL, Vol. 4*, p 286.

44. Neville Chamberlain to Hilda Chamberlain, 15 October 1937 in *NCDL, Vol. 4*, p 356.

45. Neville Chamberlain to Hilda Chamberlain, 24 October 1937 in *NCDL, Vol. 4*, p 279.

46. Neville Chamberlain to Ida Chamberlain, 12 December 1937 in *NCDL, Vol. 4*, p 290.

47. Neville Chamberlain to Hilda Chamberlain, 27 February 1938 in *NCDL, Vol. 4*, p 303.

48. Ramsden, *The Age of Balfour and Baldwin*, p 366.

49. Neville Chamberlain to Hilda Chamberlain, 21 November 1937 in *NCDL, Vol. 4*, p 284.

50. Neville Chamberlain to Ida Chamberlain, 10 November 1934 in *NCDL, Vol. 4*, p 73.

51. Neville Chamberlain to Ida Chamberlain, 23 January 1938 in *NCDL, Vol. 4*, pp 297–8; and Martin Gilbert, 'Horace Wilson: Man of Munich?', *History Today* (October 1982) p 5.

52. Neville Chamberlain to Hilda Chamberlain, 13 March 1938 in *NCDL, Vol. 4*, p 304.

53. Neville Chamberlain to Hilda Chamberlain, 13 March 1938 in *NCDL, Vol. 4*, p 304.

54. Neville Chamberlain to Ida Chamberlain, 20 March 1938 in *NCDL, Vol. 4*, p 307.
55. Neville Chamberlain to Ida Chamberlain, 20 March 1938 in *NCDL, Vol. 4*, pp 307–8.
56. Neville Chamberlain to Hilda Chamberlain, 27 March 1938 in *NCDL, Vol. 4*, p 312.
57. Neville Chamberlain to Ida Chamberlain, 16 April 1938 in *NCDL, Vol. 4*, p 316.
58. Neville Chamberlain to Ida Chamberlain, 28 May 1938 in *NCDL, Vol. 4*, p 325.
59. Neville Chamberlain to Ida Chamberlain, 1 May 1938 in *NCDL, Vol. 4*, p 318.
60. Neville Chamberlain to Ida Chamberlain, 10/15 May 1938 in *NCDL, Vol. 4*, p 321.

Chapter 5: Munich

1. Neville Chamberlain to Ida Chamberlain, 28 May 1938 in *NCDL, Vol. 4*, p 325.
2. Neville Chamberlain to Hilda Chamberlain, 25 June 1938 in *NCDL Vol. 4*, p 331.
3. Ian Kershaw, *Hitler: Nemesis, 1936–1945* (Penguin, London: 2000) pp 108–9.
4. Neville Chamberlain to Ida Chamberlain, 11 September 1938 in *NCDL, Vol. 4*, p 344.
5. Neville Chamberlain to Ida Chamberlain, 3 September 1938 in *NCDL, Vol. 4*, p 342.
6. Neville Chamberlain to Ida Chamberlain, 11 September 1938 in *NCDL, Vol. 4*, p 344.
7. Neville Chamberlain to Ida Chamberlain, 19 September 1938 in *NCDL, Vol. 4*, pp 345–9.
8. Robert Rhodes James (ed), *'Chips': The Diaries of Sir Henry Channon* (Weidenfeld & Nicolson, London: 1993) p 166.

9. Neville Chamberlain to Ida Chamberlain, 19 September 1938 in *NCDL, Vol. 4*, pp 345–9.

10. Neville Chamberlain to Ida Chamberlain, 19 September 1938 in *NCDL, Vol. 4*, p 348.

11. Neville Chamberlain to Ida Chamberlain, 19 September 1938 in *NCDL, Vol. 4*, p 348.

12. John Charmley, *Duff Cooper* (Phoenix, London: 1997) p 117.

13. Kershaw, *Hitler: Nemesis* pp 112–15.

14. Gilbert, 'Horace Wilson', p 7.

15. Kershaw, *Hitler: Nemesis*, p 116.

16. Kershaw, *Hitler: Nemesis*, p 118.

17. Neville Chamberlain to Hilda Chamberlain, 2 October 1938 in *NCDL, Vol. 4*, p 349.

18. Neville Chamberlain to Hilda Chamberlain, 2 October 1938 in *NCDL, Vol. 4*, p 349.

19. Nigel Nicolson (ed), *Harold Nicolson: Diaries and Letters, 1930–39* (Fontana, London: 1969) p 364

20. R J B Bosworth, *Mussolini* (Arnold, London: 2002) p 333.

21. Neville Chamberlain to Hilda Chamberlain, 2 October 1938 in *NCDL, Vol. 4*, p 350.

22. Kershaw, *Hitler: Nemesis*, p 121.

23. Kershaw, *Hitler: Nemesis*, pp 123–5.

24. Neville Chamberlain to Hilda Chamberlain, 2 October 1938 in *NCDL, Vol. 4*, pp 350–1.

25. Parker, *Chamberlain and Appeasement*, pp 180–1.

26. Neville Chamberlain to Hilda Chamberlain, 2 October 1938 in *NCDL, Vol. 4*, p 351.

27. Brian MacArthur (ed), *The Penguin Book of Twentieth Century Speeches* (Penguin, London: 1999) p 170.

28. Neville Chamberlain to Hilda Chamberlain, 15 October 1938 in *NCDL, Vol. 4*, p 355.

29. Neville Chamberlain to Ida Chamberlain, 24 October 1938 in *NCDL, Vol. 4*, p 358.

30. Neville Chamberlain to Hilda Chamberlain, 6 November 1938, in *NCDL, Vol. 4*, p 361.

31. Ramsden, *The Age of Balfour and Baldwin*, pp 366–7.

32. Christopher Andrew, *Her Majesty's Secret Service* (Viking, New York: 1986) p 387.

33. Richard Cockett, *Twilight of Truth: Chamberlain, Appeasement and the Manipulation of the Press* (Weidenfeld and Nicolson, London: 1989) pp 85–6.

34. Neville Chamberlain to Hilda Chamberlain, 30 December 1939 in *NCDL, Vol. 4*, p 483.

35. Stewart, *Burying Caesar*, p 346.

36. Neville Chamberlain to Hilda Chamberlain, 15 October 1938 in *NCDL, Vol. 4*, p 356.

37. Neville Chamberlain to Hilda Chamberlain, 6 November 1938, in *NCDL, Vol. 4*, p 361.

38. Neville Chamberlain to Ida Chamberlain, 13 November 1938 in *NCDL, Vol. 4*, pp 362–3.

39. Neville Chamberlain to Hilda Chamberlain, 15 January 1939 in *NCDL, Vol. 4*, pp 373–5.

40. Neville Chamberlain to Hilda Chamberlain, 11 December 1938 in *NCDL, Vol. 4*, pp 367–9.

41. Neville Chamberlain to Hilda Chamberlain, 19 February 1939 in *NCDL, Vol. 4*, p 382.

42. Neville Chamberlain to Ida Chamberlain, 5 February 1939 in *NCDL, Vol. 4*, pp 377–9.

43. Neville Chamberlain to Ida Chamberlain, 12 February 1939 in *NCDL, Vol. 4*, p 380.

Chapter 6: The Failure of Appeasement

1. Nicolson (ed), *Harold Nicolson: Diaries and Letters*, p 393.

2. Dutton, *Neville Chamberlain*, p 23.

3. Neville Chamberlain to Ida Chamberlain, 23 April 1939 in *NCDL, Vol. 4*, pp 409–10.

4. Neville Chamberlain to Ida Chamberlain, 26 March 1939 in *NCDL, Vol. 4*, pp 395–6

5. Peijan Shen, *The Age of Appeasement: The Evolution of British Foreign Policy in the 1930s* (Sutton, Stroud: 1999) p xvii.

6. Neville Chamberlain to Hilda Chamberlain, 29 April 1939 in *NCDL, Vol. 4*, p 412.

7. Neville Chamberlain to Hilda Chamberlain, 15 July 1939 in *NCDL, Vol. 4*, pp 427–30.

8. Neville Chamberlain to Hilda Chamberlain, 26 March 1939 in *NCDL, Vol. 4*, pp 396–7.

9. Neville Chamberlain to Hilda Chamberlain, 1–2 April 1939 in *NCDL, Vol. 4*, p 400.

10. Neville Chamberlain to Hilda Chamberlain, 1–2 April 1939 in *NCDL, Vol. 4*, p 401.

11. Neville Chamberlain to Hilda Chamberlain, 29 April 1939 in *NCDL, Vol. 4*, p 411.

12. Shen, *The Age of Appeasement*, pp 226–8.

13. Neville Chamberlain to Hilda Chamberlain, 27 August 1939 in *NCDL, Vol. 4*, pp 440–1.

14. Lord Blake, *The Conservative Party from Peel to Major* (Heinemann, London: 1997) p 243.

15. Richard Baker, 'Lidell, (Tord) Alvar Quan (1908–1981)', *Oxford Dictionary of National Biography* (Oxford University Press: 2004) [http://www.oxforddnb.com/view/article/31361, accessed 17 March 2006].

16. Feiling, *The Life of Neville Chamberlain*, p 416.

17. Neville Chamberlain to Ida Chamberlain, 10 September 1939 in *NCDL, Vol. 4*, pp 440–1, 443–5.

18. Neville Chamberlain to Ida Chamberlain, 23 September 1939 in *NCDL, Vol. 4*, pp 449–52.

19. Neville Chamberlain to Hilda Chamberlain, 25 February 1940 in *NCDL, Vol. 4*, p 503.

20. Feiling, *The Life of Neville Chamberlain*, p 443.

21. N J Crowson (ed), *Fleet Street, Press Barons and Politics: The Journals of Collin Brooks, 1932–1940* (Royal Historical Society/UCL, London: 1998) p 268.

22. MacLeod, *Neville Chamberlain*, p 280.

23. Neville Chamberlain to Ida Chamberlain, 11 May 1940 in *NCDL, Vol. 4*, pp 528–9

24. MacLeod, *Neville Chamberlain*, p 289.

25. Geoffrey Wheatcroft, *The Strange Death of Tory England* (Penguin, London: 2005) p 48.

26. Francis Williams, *A Prime Minister Remembers: The War and Post-War Memoirs of the Rt. Hon. Earl Attlee* (Heinemann, London: 1961) p 33.

27. Neville Chamberlain to Ida Chamberlain, 11 May 1940 in *NCDL, Vol. 4*, pp 528–9.

28. Andrew Roberts, *'The Holy Fox': The Life of Lord Halifax* (Phoenix, London: 1991) p 208.

29. John Lukacs, *Five Days in London: May 1940* (Yale University Press, London: 1999) p 17.

30. Neville Chamberlain to Hilda Chamberlain, 17 May 1940 in *NCDL, Vol. 4*, pp 531–2

31. John Ramsden, *The Age of Balfour and Baldwin*, p 373.

32. David Dilks, 'The Twilight of War and the Fall of France: Chamberlain and Churchill in 1940', in David Dilks (ed) *Retreat From Power: Studies in Britain's Foreign Policy in the Twentieth Century, Vol. Two: After 1939* (Macmillan, London: 1981) pp 36–65.

33. Williams, *A Prime Minister Remembers*, p 37.

34. Paul Addison, *The Road to 1945* (Pimlico, London: 1994) p 113.

35. Winston Churchill to Neville Chamberlain, 30 September and reply, 1 October 1940 quoted in *NCDL, Vol. 4*, p 47

36. Rhodes James (ed), *'Chips'*, p 275.

37. *The Times*, 11 November 1940.

Chapter 7: Chamberlain and the Battle for History

1. Norman Davies, *Europe: A History* (Pimlico, London: 1997) p 990.

2. H M Hyde, *Neville Chamberlain* (Weidenfeld and Nicolson, London: 1976) p 169.

3. Andrew J Crozier, 'Chamberlain, (Arthur) Neville (1869–1940), *Oxford Dictionary of National Biography* (Oxford University Press: 2004) [http://www.oxforddnb.com/view/article/32347, accessed 8 April 2006].

4. Dutton, *Neville Chamberlain*, p 193

5. Ramsden, *The Age of Balfour and Baldwin*, p 372.

6. *The Times*, 13 November 1940.

7. Dutton, *Neville Chamberlain*, p 184.

8. Neville Chamberlain to Hilda Chamberlain, 1 June 1940 in *NCDL Vol. 4*, p 535.

9. Addison, *The Road to 1945*, pp 110–12.

10. Neville Chamberlain to Ida Chamberlain, 20 July 1940 in *NCDL Vol. 4*, p 553.

11. Ramsden, *The Age of Balfour and Baldwin*, p 374.

12. Williams, *A Pattern of Rulers*, p 193.

13. *The Times*, 7 November 1940.

14. Dutton, *Neville Chamberlain*, p 189.

15. Dutton, *Neville Chamberlain*, p 70.

16. Neville Chamberlain to Joseph Ball, 28 October 1940 quoted in *NCDL Vol. 4*, p 48.
17. *The Times*, 11 November 1940.
18. Dutton, *Neville Chamberlain*, pp 79, 129–30
19. Feiling and Dutton, *Neville Chamberlain*, pp 123–9.
20. Nigel Fisher, *Ian MacLeod* (Andre Deutsch, London: 1973) p 211.
21. David Reynolds, *In Command of History: Churchill Fighting and Writing the Second World War* (Penguin, London: 2005) pp 32–3.
22. MacLeod, *Neville Chamberlain*, p 304.
23. Robert Self, 'Introduction', *NCDL Vol. 4*, p 7.
24. John Charmley, *Chamberlain and the Lost Peace* (Hodder and Stoughton, London: 1989) p 212.
25. Dutton, *Neville Chamberlain*, p 166.
26. John Charmley, *Churchill: The End of Glory* (Harcourt, London: 1993) p 2.
27. John Lukacs, *Churchill: Visionary, Statesman, Historian* (Yale University Press, London: 2002) pp 150–4.
28. Aster, ' "Guilty Men": The Case of Neville Chamberlain,' in Boyce and Robertson (eds), *Paths to War: New Essays on the Origins of the Second World War*, pp 241 and 262.
29. Parker, *Chamberlain and Appeasement*, p 347.
30. *The Times*, 25 October 1993.
31. R A C Parker, *Churchill and Appeasement* (Macmillan, London: 2000) pp 258–64.
32. John Lukacs, *Churchill: Visionary, Statesman, Historian* (Yale University Press, London: 2002) pp 119–20.
33. Dutton, *Neville Chamberlain*, pp 165 and 184.

Chapter 8: An Assessment

1. Dutton, *Neville Chamberlain*, p 209.

2. David Dilks, 'Appeasement and "Intelligence,"' in Dilks (ed) *Retreat from Power Vol 1*, p 143.

3. Michael Howard, 'British Military Preparations for the Second World War,' in Dilks (ed), *Retreat From Power Vol 1*, pp 102–17.

4. Howard, 'British Military Preparations', pp 106–7.

5. Robert Self, 'Introduction', *The Neville Chamberlain Diary Letters, Vol. 4*, p 29.

6. Robert Shay, *British Rearmament in the Thirties: Politics and Profits* (Princeton University Press, Princeton: 1977) p 165.

7. Shay, *British Rearmament* pp 284, 286.

8. Robert Self, 'Introduction', *NCDL Vol. 4*, pp 30–1.

9. Dutton, *Neville Chamberlain*, p 173.

10. Neville Chamberlain to Ida Chamberlain, 8 December 1935 in *NCDL Vol. 4*, p 165.

11. Dutton, *Neville Chamberlain*, pp 177–8.

12. Shay, *British Rearmament*, pp 284–5.

13. David Dilks, '"The Unnecessary War"? Military Advice and Foreign Policy in Great Britain, 1931–1939,' in Adrian Preston (ed), *General Staffs and Diplomacy before the Second World War* (Croon Helm, London: 1978) p 117.

14. Sean Greenwood, '"Caligula's Horse" Revisited: Sir Thomas Inskip as Minister for the Co-Ordination of Defence, 1936–1939', *Journal of Strategic Studies*, 17, 2 (1994).

15. Dilks, 'The Unnecessary War', pp 125–6.

16. Addison, *The Road to 1945*, p 112.

17. Shay, *British Rearmament*, pp 186–294.

18. Greenwood, '"Caligula's Horse" Revisited'.

19. Howard, 'British Military Preparations for the Second World War', pp 102–17.

20. Feiling, *The Life of Neville Chamberlain*, p 324.
21. Dutton, *Neville Chamberlain*, pp 218–19.
22. The Late Lord Strang, 'The Moscow Negotiations, 1939,' in Dilks (ed), *Retreat From Power Vol. 1*, pp 170–86.
23. A J P Taylor, *The Origins of the Second World War* (Penguin, London: 1961) p 229.
24. Richard Lamb, *Mussolini and the British* (John Murray, London: 1997) pp 180–99.
25. Norton Medlicott, 'Britain and Germany: The Search for Agreement, 1930–1937', in David Dilks (ed), *Retreat From Power Vol. 1*, pp 78–101.
26. B J C McKercher, 'The Foreign Office, 1930–1939: Strategy, Permanent Interests and National Security', *Contemporary British History*, 18, 3 (Autumn 2004) pp 87–109.
27. Gilbert, 'Horace Wilson: Man of Munich?', p 6.
28. Christopher Andrew, 'Secret Intelligence and British Foreign Policy, 1900–1939', in Christopher Andrew and Jeremy Noakes (eds), *Intelligence and International Relations, 1900–1945* (Exeter University Press, Exeter: 1987) pp 9–28.
29. Michael Howard, 'British Military Preparations', pp 113–14.
30. David Dilks (ed), *The Diaries of Sir Alexander Cadogan* (Cassell, London: 1971) p 63.
31. Andrew, 'Secret Intelligence and British Foreign Policy', pp 9–28.
32. Stewart, *Burying Caesar*, pp 310–18.
33. F H Hinsley *et al*, *British Intelligence in the Second World War* (HMSO, London: 1979) p 82.

34. Chamberlain made almost identical remarks to Sir Horace Wilson during the flight itself, see Dutton, *Neville Chamberlain*, p 170.

35. Dilks, 'The Unnecessary War', p 113.

36. Reynolds, *In Command of History*, p 99.

37. Dutton, *Neville Chamberlain*, p 173.

38. Dilks, 'Appeasement and "Intelligence', pp 139–201.

39. Wesley K Wark, *The Ultimate Enemy: British Intelligence and Nazi Germany, 1933–1939* (Oxford University Press, Oxford: 1986); and Andrew, 'Secret Intelligence and British Foreign Policy', pp 9–28.

40. *The Times*, 7 November 1940.

41. Dutton, *Neville Chamberlain*, p 194.

42. Stewart, *Burying Caesar*, pp 310–18.

43. Dilks, 'The Twilight of War and the Fall of France: Chamberlain and Churchill in 1940,' in Dilks (ed) *Retreat From Power Vol. 2: After 1939*, pp 43–4, 64.

44. David Dilks, 'Appeasement and "Intelligence', in Dilks (ed) *Retreat from Power Vol 1*, p 165.

45. Andrew, *Her Majesty's Secret Service*, p 397.

46. Parker, *Chamberlain and Appeasement*, p 343.

47. Dutton, *Neville Chamberlain*, p 211.

CHRONOLOGY

Year	Premiership
1937	28 May: Neville Chamberlain becomes Prime Minister, aged 68.
	Lord Halifax attempts settlement of Sudetenland problem with Hitler.
	The Factory Act sought to improve working conditions but limiting working hours for women and children and setting standard working regulations.
	Physical Training Act.
1938	February: Eden resigns as Foreign Secretary.
	April: Anglo-Italian agreement is signed, recognising Mussolini's conquest of Abyssinia in return for the withdrawal of 'volunteers' from Spain.
	September: Chamberlain, on his third trip to Germany for talks to avert war, signs the Munich Agreement.
	The Housing Act provided subsidies that encouraged slum clearance, as well as maintaining rent control.
	The Coal Act: coal deposits were to be nationalised and a Coal Commission was established to administer them.
	Holidays with Pay Act.
1939	March: Chamberlain guarantees Polish sovereignty.
	Conscription introduced.
	3 September: Britain declares war on Germany following invasion of Poland.
	Churchill appointed First Lord of the Admiralty.
	British Expeditionary Force sent to France.
	October: First German air raid on Britain.
	December: The Battle of the River Plate: *Graf Spee* scuttled.
1940	April: German invasion of Norway. Allied troops sent to Narvik six days later.
	8 May: Government majority in vote of confidence in Norway debate drops to only 81 votes.
	10 May: Chamberlain resigns after two years and 348 days in office, on the same day as Germany invades Holland and Belgium.

History	Culture
Japan invades China. UK royal commission on Palestine recommends partition into British and Arab areas and Jewish state. Italy joins Anti-Comintern Pact. Frank Whittle invents jet engine.	George Orwell, *The Road to Wigan Pier*. Fernand Leger, *Le Transport des Forces*. Picasso, *Guernica*. John Steinbeck, *Of Mice and Men*. Nylon patented in USA. Films: *Snow White and the Seven Dwarfs*. *A Star is Born*.
German troops enter Austria which is declared part of the German Reich. Japanese puppet government of China at Nanjing. Anti-Semitic legislation in Italy; no public employment or property. Kristallnacht in Germany – Jewish houses, synagogues and schools burnt for a week. Nuclear fission discovered in Germany.	J B Huizinga, *Homo Ludens*. Frank Lloyd Wright, Taliesen West, Phoenix, USA. Graham Greene, *Brighton Rock*. Evelyn Waugh, *Scoop*. *Picture Post* founded in Britain. Films: *Pygmalion*. *Alexander Nevsky*. *The Adventures of Robin Hood*.
Germans troops enter Prague. Italy invades Albania. Germany demands Danzig and Polish Corridor. Poland refuses. Spanish Civil War ends. Japanese-Soviet clashes in Manchuria. Pact of Steel signed by Hitler and Mussolini. Nazi-Soviet pact signed. Soviets invade Finland.	Bela Bartok, *String Quartet No. 6*. James Joyce, *Finnegan's Wake*. Thomas Mann, *Lotte in Weimar*. John Steinbeck, *The Grapes of Wrath*. Films: *Gone with the Wind*. *Goodbye Mr Chips*. *The Wizard of Oz*.
Finnish-Soviet 'Winter War ends. Japanese set up puppet government in Manchuria.	Graham Greene, *The Power and the Glory*. Ernest Hemingway, *For Whom the Bell Tolls*. Films: *The Great Dictator*. *Pinocchio*. *Rebecca*.

FURTHER READING

Neville Chamberlain died without leaving an autobiography. His personal papers are deposited at the University of Birmingham. However, for those wishing to enjoy the insights into his personal and political life these papers provide without travelling to the Midlands will find that consulting the four volumes of *The Neville Chamberlain Diary Letters* (Ashgate, Aldershot: 2000–2005) edited by Robert Self and which span Chamberlain's political life from 1915 to 1940, indispensable. Similarly illumination can be found in Robert Self (ed), *The Austen Chamberlain Diary Letters* (Royal Historical Society/CUP, Cambridge: 1995), which provides some interesting insights into Chamberlain's early political career from the perspective of his half-brother, Austen.

An absolutely indispensable guide to Chamberlain that charts the changing fortunes of his historical reputation is David Dutton's *Neville Chamberlain* (Arnold, London: 2001), which provides a magnificent overview of both of the history and historiography and is therefore warmly recommended. John Ramsden, *The Age of Balfour and Baldwin, 1902–1940* (Longman, London: 1978) provides a most invaluable overview of Conservative Party politics during this period.

In many ways the first authorised biography of Chamberlain by Keith Feiling, *The Life of Neville Chamberlain* (Macmillan, London: 1946), although overtly sympathetic to its subject, remains the best. Later efforts at biography including *Neville Chamberlain* (Frederick Muller, London: 1961) by Ian MacLeod, and H M Hyde, *Neville Chamberlain* (Weidenfeld and Nicolson, London: 1976) are still useful, however. Andrew Crozier who penned Chamberlain's entry in the *Oxford Dictionary of National Biography* is currently preparing a full-length study of Chamberlain, which is eagerly awaited.

The memoirs of many of Chamberlain's close colleagues provide a wealth of information on Chamberlain's personality and working methods as well as defences for his policies. Foremost amongst these are Lord Templewood, *Nine Troubled Years* (Collins, London: 1954), R A Butler, *The Art of the Possible: The Memoirs of Lord Butler* (Hamish Hamilton, London: 1971), Earl Swinton, *Sixty Years of Power: Some Memories of the Men who wielded it* (Hutchinson, London: 1966), Viscount Simon, *Retrospect* (Hutchinson, London: 1952), and Herbert Samuel, *Memoirs* (Cressett Press, London: 1945). From the other side Francis Williams, *A Prime Minister Remembers: The War and Post-War Memoirs of the Rt. Hon. Earl Attlee* (Heinemann, London: 1961) provides a number of interesting observations, as do the memoirs of other Labour leaders during this period. A very useful short study of Chamberlain's close confidant Sir Horace Wilson is Martin Gilbert, 'Horace Wilson: Man of Munich?' *History Today* (October 1982).

Numerous fascinating insights can be gained from the plethora of diaries kept by Chamberlain's political contemporaries. Foremost amongst these are the two-volume *The Headlam Diaries* (Historians Press, London: 1992) edited by Stuart Ball which give a unique backbench northern view of Chamberlain's political career. Phillip Williamson (ed), *The Modernisation of Conservative Politics: The Diaries and Letters of William Bridgeman, 1904–1935* (Historians' Press, London: 1988) is similarly useful in this respect. Robert Rhodes James (ed), *Memoirs of a Conservative* (Weidenfeld & Nicolson, London: 1969) provide some similarly informative observations by the chairman of the Conservative Party J C C Davidson who was displaced by Chamberlain. John Colville, *The Fringes of Power* (Hodder and Stoughton, London: 1985) is similarly useful. Also useful for their gossipy asides are Nigel Nicolson (ed), *Harold Nicolson: Diaries and Letter, 1930–39* (Fontana, London: 1969) as well as Robert Rhodes James (ed), *'Chips': The Diaries of Sir Henry Channon* (Weidenfeld & Nicolson, London: 1993), which although sycophantic is entertaining if nothing else.

The animosity Chamberlain felt for Lloyd George be gleaned from *The Neville Chamberlain Diary Letters* and is equally evident in David Lloyd George, *War Memoirs: Vol. 3* (Odhams Press, London: 1934) and Kevin O Morgan (ed.), *Lloyd George: Family Letters, 1885–1936* (Oxford University Press, Oxford: 1973). Stuart Ball, 'The Conservative Party and the Formation of the National Government: August 1931', *The Historical Journal*, 29, 1 (1986) provides detailed information on the formation of the National Government which refutes the premise that it was deliberately engineered by Chamberlain to besmirch the Labour government, though this was one of its effects.

The first concerted attempt to rehabilitate Chamberlain's political life was made by John Charmley, *Chamberlain and the Lost Peace* (Hodder and Stoughton, London: 1989) which was followed by *Churchill: The End of Glory* (Harcourt, London: 1993). Almost simultaneously a 'post-revisionist' school of literature has developed in the vanguard of which is Sidney Aster, ' "Guilty Men": The Case of Neville Chamberlain' in Robert Boyce and Esmonde M Robertson (eds), *Paths to War: New Essays on the Origins of the Second World War* (St Martins Press, London: 1989). The case against revisionism is most persuasively put in R A C Parker, *Chamberlain and Appeasement* (Macmillan, London: 1993), which argues that Chamberlain did indeed have alternatives from which he could have chosen. Parker explores these some of these alternatives in *Churchill and Appeasement* (Macmillan, London: 2000).

The crucial financial dimension to appeasement is articulated in Robert Shay, *British Rearmament in the Thirties: Politics and Profits* (Princeton University Press, Princeton: 1977). Sean Greenwood, '"Caligula's Horse" Revisited: Sir Thomas Inskip as Minister for the Co-Ordination of Defence, 1936–1939,' *Journal of Strategic Studies*, 17, 2 (1994) is similarly useful in its examination of how the Chamberlain administration sought to rationalise and co-ordinate British defence after 1936. Michael Howard, 'British Military Preparations for the Second World War,' in David Dilks (ed), *Retreat From Power: Studies in Britain's Foreign Policy of the Twentieth Century, Vol. One, 1906–1939* (Macmillan, London: 1981) provides an in depth study of the military strategy underpinning Chamberlain's policies as does David Dilks, '"The Unnecessary War"? Military Advice and Foreign Policy in Great Britain, 1931–1939,' in Adrian Preston (ed), *General Staffs and Diplomacy before the Second World War* (Croon Helm, London: 1978). How the 'missing dimension' of British intelligence shaped appeasement is charted in Wesley K Wark, *The Ultimate Enemy: British Intelligence and Nazi Germany, 1933–1939* (Oxford University Press, Oxford: 1986) as well as in David Dilks, 'Appeasement and "Intelligence"', in David Dilks (ed) *Retreat from Power: Studies in Britain's Foreign Policy of the Twentieth Century, Volume One, 1906–1939* (Macmillan, London: 1981). Still useful is Christopher Andrew, *Her Majesty's Secret Service* (Viking, New York: 1986). The Colonial aspect of appeasement is explored in Andrew J Crozier, *Appeasement and Germany's Last Bid for Colonies* (Macmillan, London: 1988) whilst Peijan Shen, *The Age of Appeasement* (Sutton, Stroud: 1999) emphasises the too often ignored Japanese dimension of appeasement. Those interested in the Italian dimension of appeasement can profitably consult Richard Lamb, *Mussolini and the British* (John Murray, London: 1997) whilst those seeking insights into Hitler's view of the 'worms' of Munich should consult the second volume of Sir Ian Kershaw's magisterial biography *Hitler: Nemesis, 1936–1945* (Penguin, London: 2000).

Chamberlain's foreign secretary Anthony Eden belatedly gave his version of events in *The Eden Memoirs* (Cassell, London: 1962), though of far more use is David Dutton, *Anthony Eden: A Life and Reputation* (Arnold, London: 1997). Andrew Roberts' study of Eden's replacement *'The Holy Fox': The Life of Lord Halifax* (Arnold, London: 1991) is similarly useful for the insights it provides into another of the foremost proponents of appeasement. The 'anti-appeasement' view of the Foreign Office is articulated in Lord Vansittart, *The Mist Procession* (Hutchinson, London: 1958).

Chamberlain's attempts to manipulate the press as a means of promoting appeasement are dealt with in Richard Cockett, *Twilight of Truth: Chamberlain, Appeasement and the Manipulation of the Press* (Weidenfeld and Nicolson, London: 1989) whilst additional light on his use of *Truth* to smear political opponents can be found in *Fleet Street, Press Barons and Politics: The Journals of Collin Brooks, 1932–1940* (Royal Historical Society/UCL, London: 1998) edited by N J Crowson.

Burying Caesar: The Churchill-Chamberlain Rivalry (Overlook Press, New York: 2001) by Graham Stewart provides a fascinating study of these two intertwined political careers. John Lukacs, *Five Days in London: May 1940* (Yale University Press, London: 1999) paints a fascinating portrait of Chamberlain's fall and Churchill's assumption of power. David Dilks, 'The Twilight of War and the Fall of France: Chamberlain and Churchill in 1940', in David Dilks (ed), *Retreat From Power: Studies in Britain's Foreign Policy in the Twentieth Century, Vol. Two: After 1939* (Macmillan, London: 1981) is crucial to understanding the close working relationship that developed between Churchill and Chamberlain after the latter's fall in May 1940. Absolutely indispensable to understanding how Churchill helped to shape Chamberlain's historical reputation is David Reynolds, *In Command of History: Churchill Fighting and Writing the Second World War* (Penguin, London: 2005)

Picture Sources

Page vi
Chamberlain and Adolf Hitler meet at Berchtesgaden, 15
September 1938. (Courtesy Topham Picturepoint)

Pages 92–3
Chamberlain photographed on his return from Germany
displaying the signed peace accord to the assembled Press
Corps. (Courtesy Topham Picturepoint)

Pages 132–3
Chamberlain and Hitler photographed in Bad Godesberg
after talks over the Sudeten crisis, 23 September 1938.
(Courtesy akg Images)

Index